AN ORKNEY TAPESTRY 'is a spectrum of lore, legend and literature, a highly coloured reaction as Orkney breaks open in the prisms of a poet's mind and memory' – Seamus Heaney, *The Listener*

'George Mackay Brown is a portent. No one else writes like this or has this feeling for language. No one else stands out against the gravel background of modern literature with forms and colours like those he has taken from Orkney and made his own. His is an innate talent: as true as that of Yeats' – Jo Grimmond, *Spectator*

George Mackay Brown is one of Scotland's most gifted poets and short story writers, whose work is universally acclaimed. He lives in Stromness, where he has always lived: *An Orkney Tapestry* is his testimonial to his native land.

The drawings in this book are by the Orcadian artist Sylvia Wishart.

AN ORKNEY TAPESTRY

GEORGE MACKAY BROWN

with drawings by Sylvia Wishart

QUARTET BOOKS
LONDON MELBOURNE NEW YORK

Published by Quartet Books Limited 1973
A member of the Namara Group
27 Goodge Street, London W1P 1FD
Reprinted 1974, 1978

First published in Great Britain by
Victor Gollancz Limited 1969
Reprinted 1972

ISBN 0 7043 3083 0

Printed in Great Britain by
Hunt Barnard Printing Ltd, Aylesbury, Bucks

To Charles and Carol Senior

ILLUSTRATIONS
Between pages 102 and 103

ORKNEY

FOREWORD

To WRITE a new book on Orkney is no easy matter. Nearly every facet of life in the islands has been described and discussed and catalogued over and over again: the towns and villages, the churches, the fields and waters and skies, the animals, the birds, the shells, the rocks, the weather, the old stones, the language and the place-names, big islands and small holms – above all the people, 'their gear and tackle and trim'.

Most writers on Orkney have been practical in their approach. Excellent studies have been published – Hugh Marwick's *Orkney Norn* and *Orkney Farm Names*; Robert Rendall's *Mollusca Orcadensia*; Storer Clouston's *History of Orkney*; John Firth's *Reminiscences of an Orkney Parish*; and many others.

A few poets – Walter Traill Dennison, Edwin Muir, Robert Rendall (he was that rare kind of being, poet as well as scholar) – have been more interested in essences; they have described the vision by which the people live, what Edwin Muir called their Fable.

This book takes its stand with the poets. I am interested in facts only as they tend and gesture, like birds and grass and waves, in 'the gale of life'. I have tried to make a kind of profile of Orkney, which is not a likeness of today only; it has been worked on for many centuries. 'I lean my cheek from eternity . . .'

The facts of our history – what Edwin Muir called The Story – are there to read and study: the neolithic folk, Picts, Norsemen, Scots, the slow struggle of the people towards independence and prosperity. But it often seems that history is only the forging, out of terrible and kindly fires, of a mask. The mask is undeniably there; it is impressive and reassuring, it flatters us to wear it.

Underneath, the true face dreams on, and The Fable is repeated over and over again.

I have had to wrench skaldic verse into a shape acceptable to modern readers. Any attempt to reproduce something like the original is impossibly difficult; the Vikings' poetry is not poetry as we understand it. A. B. Taylor, in his translation of *The Orkneyinga Saga* – which I have read with delight many times – gives Armod's poem, on shipwatch, off Crete, like this:

> We watch o'er the sea-steed
> While o'er the stout gun-wale
> The billow breaks wildly.
> Thus duty is done.
> While the lazy land-lubber
> Sleeps by some maiden
> Soft-skinned and kind,
> Over my shoulder
> I gaze towards Crete.

It is doubtless a faithful rendering. But wouldn't the Norsemen who heard the poem for the first time next morning have been delighted, much as Ayrshire farmers when Burns recited *Go Bring to me a Pint o' Wine* to them? I expect no delight at all for my very free paraphrase; only that perhaps it is more in accord with modern taste; so with all the verse renderings in the 'Crusader' chapter.

> Night. Sheets of salt.
> Armod on watch.
> A heave and wash of lights from the island.
> The lads of Crete
> Toss in hot tumbled linen.
> This poet on watch,
> Cold, burning, unkissed.

I have used poet's licence with the translations of the saga, especially in the 'Martyr' chapter, in order to round out a meaning.

Edwin Muir is a more important poet than Robert Rendall; some readers will think I should have chosen to write about him. But much study has been devoted to Muir, and there will be more books about him and his poetry in the years to come. Robert Rendall is a fine poet who has been neglected. Half a dozen lyrics from *Orkney Variants* hold most of the essence of Orkney.

In the 'Rackwick' chapter some of my own poems are included. They are taken from a long unfinished sequence called *Fishermen with Ploughs*. Some of those in the present book have appeared in *The Scotsman* and *Transatlantic Review* and have been broadcast in the Third Programme. Poems in other chapters have appeared in *The Listener* and *Extra Verse*.

The book tries to recount some of the events and imaginings that have made the Orkney people what they are, in a sequence of vivid patterns: as women with looms and coloured wools sat in the earl's hall and wove the events surrounding Hastings, perhaps, or The Stations of the Cross. The predominant web-imagery of the *Warrior* and *Martyr* chapters finally decided the title.

My thanks especially to Mr Ernest W. Marwick, who read over my manuscripts and proofs and, out of his deep knowledge of the islands, made many helpful suggestions. I have mined deeply from his *Anthology of Orkney Verse*: in particular I have tried to resurrect a great unknown ballad, *TheLady Odivere*, which I first read there. My thanks also to Mr Robert Rendall, East Kilbride, for permission to quote extensively from his uncle's poetry; to Messrs Faber & Faber and Mrs Willa Muir to quote from Edwin Muir's *The Ring*; to Mr George Scott- Moncrieff to quote from *Brig o' Waith*, by Ann Scott-Moncrieff; and to Mrs Nan Butcher for deciphering and typing a difficult manuscript.

Sylvia Wishart's drawings evoke beautifully the Orkney landscape; they have much enriched the text.

The play *The Watcher* was suggested by Tolstoy's marvellous story, *What Men Live By*; otherwise they are as different as a skerry from a steppe.

I

ISLANDS AND PEOPLE

ISLANDS AND PEOPLE

THERE IS the Pentland Firth to cross, first of all. This is looked on as a fearsome experience by some people who are visiting Orkney for the first time. In Scrabster they sip brandy or swallow sea-sick tablets. The crossing can be rough enough – the Atlantic and the North Sea invading each other's domain twice a day, raging back and fore through the narrow channels and sounds, an external wrestle; and the fickle wind can be foe or ally. But as often as not the Firth is calm; the *St Ola* dips through a gentle swell between Scrabster and Stromness. George Bernard Shaw visited Orkney once in the nineteen-twenties. He was impressed by that mighty outpouring of waters. There was power enough in the Pentland Firth, he wrote, to provide all Europe with electrical power. A pair of millstones at the bottom of the Firth grind the salt that makes the sea the way it is; the maelstrom called The Swelkie whirls above the place where the querns forever turn (or so the old people believed).

The cliffs of western Hoy rise up, pillars of flame. This coast has some of the tallest cliff-faces in the world, St John's Head, The Kame, The Berry, Rora Head: magnificent presences. There among them, standing out to sea a little, is the rock-stack called The Old Man of Hoy; very famous now since a team of climbers tackled it before television cameras in 1967, and got to the summit after sleeping a night in the bird-fretted crannies. An imposing presence; but from some aspects the Old Man looks comical, with his top hat and frock coat, like a Victorian gentleman, the last of the lairds turning his back on Orkney.

The Kame of Hoy, and Black Craig in the south-west of the main island, are the wide pillars of the doorway. The ferry-boat turns between them into Hoy Sound, past the green island of Graemsay with its two lighthouses, the dumpy octagon and slim dazzling cylinder. Small brown-and-green humps appear, Cava and Fara, the Scapa Flow islands; and the hills of Orphir. A tall iron beacon, wanly winking, stands in the tide-race. The *St Ola* turns into Stromness harbour. The engines shut off. The boat glides towards the pier, the gulls, the waiting faces.

This is one way to arrive in Orkney.

Another way is to take one of the cargo-and-passenger boats from Leith or Aberdeen. That way, you arrive in Orkney in darkness. You wake up and already dockers are busy at the cargo. Through a port-hole you can see a bustling waterfront. This is Kirkwall, the commercial and adminis-trative centre of the islands.

Or, if it's speed you're after, you can drop out of the clouds on to Grimsetter runway by B.E.A. This is not the best way to get a first favourable impression. A gloom of moorland and low hills lies all about the airport. But after three miles the bus tops a rise and Kirkwall is spread out beneath, between its own bay and the most famous of all war-time anchorages, Scapa Flow. From the heart of the town rises the twelfth-century church of Saint Magnus the Martyr. It is, after all, a good way to arrive.

Scapa Flow, as the name implies, has been an anchorage

since the first longships came out of the east, and possibly earlier. That quiet stretch of water suddenly became the most famous anchorage in the world in July 1914, when the ships of the British Navy took up their silent stations there; issuing out only once to do battle, at Jutland in 1916. In 1916 also Kitchener sailed from Scapa Flow to his death in the *Hampshire*, round the corner, off Marwick Head. In 1919 a boat-load of children, out of Stromness on a school treat, saw the suicide of the German High Fleet, warship after warship filling and heeling over; the children clapped their hands and cheered at the lavish treat that had been laid on for them . . . In the Second World War, Scapa Flow was still important enough to be a target for bombers and submarines. The most famous victim was the *Royal Oak*, sunk with four daring midnight torpedoes. Bombs fall everywhere; in the little hamlet of Bridge-of-Waithe was killed the first civilian of the Second World War, standing in his doorway. Ann Scott-Moncrieff wrote a poem about that night.

> . . . They were
> Flying doon the twa lochs
> Following the sheen o' the water
> – Dost thoo mind? Ah, that time o' night –
> And they winned at last to the brig,
> Wide Waith that wreaths the salt tide wi' the fresh,
> Whaur swan and eider sweem,
> Whaur weed meets ware.
> It's no a bonny place, nither here nor there,
> Twa-three hooses and a dull-like shore . . .
>
> Here John Isbister got his death,
> Maggie o' Cumminness wi' many more
> Fearful running to the door
> Were stricken doon by door itsell,
> Wall o' hoose, bombazement, shell,
> The flying stove, the studdering road . . .

9

Kirkwall is a prosperous market town with about 5,000 people in it, a quarter of the total Orkney population. The town has many fine old buildings, one of them a jewel of great price: Saint Magnus Cathedral. It is beautiful, in spite of a clutter of plaques and memorials – the Victorians worshipped themselves in Orkney too. It stands in the centre of the islands, splashed with the red of martyrdom, and the years and the generations fall behind it. Unmoving still, it voyages on, the great ark of the people of Orkney, into unknown centuries.

Monday is the market day in Kirkwall, and the farmers come in from the parishes in their cars. There is no longer a typical Orkney farmer or farmer's wife; year by year they tend to look more like the town people. But you can still see an old countryman in Kirkwall on a Monday morning; he has red polished cheeks, he looks awkward in his best suit, he speaks in a slow rich wondering lilt, the sentences rising and breaking off at the crest: a good language for narrative and dialogue. In Scotland when people congregate they tend to argue and discuss and reason; in Orkney they tell stories.

'Ah', said the Hoy minister, consoling an eighty-year-old crofter whose wife had just worn away – 'ah, now, Jacob, look at it this way – the Lord hath given and the Lord hath taken away . . .'

Jacob considered for a while.

'Weel', said he at last, 'what could be fairer nor that?'

The authorities in Kirkwall got to know about one old woman who sold whisky of her own making without a licence, in her peedie place among the hills. An exciseman wandered as if by chance to her croft and asked for a refreshment. A cup of hill-distilled spirit was put before him. He laid a sovereign on the table and drank the wild grey stuff down, and waited for a long time for his change. 'Na', said the old body, when she got to know that he was lingering on for, 'what I gi'es I gi'es, and what I gets I keeps.'

'We'd do weel to pray,' said a North Ronaldsay fisherman to his crew as another huge wave broke over them.

It had been a fine day when they launched the boat. Then this sudden gale got up.

Willag was a kirk elder. The skipper told him to start praying.

Spindrift lashed in and over.

'O Lord,' said Willag, 'Thou are just, Thou art wonderful, Thou are merciful, great are Thy words, Thou art mighty'. Willag faltered in his litany of praise.

The boat wallowed through a huge trough.

'Butter Him up!' cried the skipper. 'Butter Him up!'

Two Flotta brothers worked their croft together. They didn't have much to say to one another.

One of them got tired of the hard drudgery. One day he slipped off without saying a thing to his brother. He enlisted in Stromness for the Hudson's Bay Company He was in Canada for a dozen years, as trapper and whaler. He got tired of that hard drudgery and decided to come home. He got a passage one autumn.

He arrived back in Flotta. His brother was sitting at the croft fire. He went in at the door.

'And mercy', said the stay-at-home, 'whare are thu been all this time?'

'Oot,' he said.

*

'Come back,' cried the fierce young woman from the end of a Hamnavoe pier. 'Come back and pay for thee bairn.'

She was shouting across the water to Andrew. Andrew had fathered her child, but had refused to acknowledge it.

Now Andrew was in the harbour, rowing the skipper of his ship – a very dignified old man – to shore.

The fierce young woman hoped to shame Andrew before his captain. 'Pay for thee bairn!' she cried.

Andrew turned to the skipper. 'Sir,' he said, 'there's a young lady on that pier over there who appears to be addressing you.'

The parish of Harray is the only parish in Orkney that has no seaboard. So Harray men are supposed to be very ignorant of the sea.

A Harray-man called Mansie was going to Hamnavoe when he saw a crab on the road – a shell with monstrous claws that slithered diagonally across the road towards him.

Mansie backed away.

'Let be for let be,' cried Mansie.

Alfred, Duke of Edinburgh, Queen Victoria's son, in his naval uniform, a splendour of gold-and-blue, attended by a glitter of officers, decided to see Maeshowe.

The old caretaker showed His Royal Highness the great stone dome, the tombs, the runic writings.

A young lieutenant of the retinue, thinking to awe the old man, whispered to him that the fine gentleman was the son of Queen Victoria, no less.

The caretaker turned to the prince. 'And what way does thee mother the queen keep?' he said. 'She's a fine aald body, deed is she. Tell her I was asking for her, be sure noo.'

All the Orcadians had a grave mild wondering speech a

generation ago; except of course the professional people – doctors and ministers – most of whom came from the south. But in the towns the shop-keepers began to use a clipped curt basic speech, as if they were imitating business letters, and now this has become increasingly the dominant kind of speech. But in the Kirkwall Mart on a Monday morning, or in a Stromness pub where the older fishermen sit at the beer tables, or in the remoter islands – Westray and Hoy – the fine original speech can still be heard; the slow laconic surging sentences; the few words considerately placed like stones on a dyke.

Farmers and crofters were poor a generation ago, but their poverty was not like urban poverty. They had as little money as the poor of Glasgow; their wealth was in their few acres and animals and children. There was always meat and drink in a farm house – the bere bannocks and butter, the dried cuithes, the white cheese, the home-brewed ale – and towards strangers a hospitality almost boundless.

The fishermen sold their haddocks along the street in the nineteen-thirties at threepence a pound. If anything, they were even poorer, living in their little houses above the harbour water, with nothing between them and hunger, between them and drowning, but a yawl.

Nowadays the people are much better off. The farms have been mechanised; land which formerly it was impossible to cultivate has been brought under the plough all over Orkney. A first glance will show how fertile the islands are – a chequer-work of pasture and cultivation from the shore half-way up the hills. The fishermen have bigger boats; they can fish in moderately deep water. They have their own co-operative and so get a secure price for their cod and lobsters and scallops. The life and prosperity of fishermen have always been more uncertain than the farmers'; probably it must be that way.

The Orcadians are people of high intelligence. The late Compton Mackenzie rated them the most intelligent people in

Britain. It has been said that the main exports are whisky and eggs and professors. This is not altogether a joke. Round about the turn of the century there was an extraordinary flowering of intellect in the islands, especially in Kirkwall Grammar School under a fierce talented dominie called Dr McEwen, though the Stromness school provided its quota too. In the course of a few years a stream of brilliant students out of Orkney passed through the universities; James Drever, later Professor of Psychology at Edinburgh; John Tait, Professor of Physiology at McGill, Canada; John Bews, Professor of Botany at Natal, South Africa, and later Principal; George Scarth, Professor of Botany at McGill; Robert Wallace, Professor of Geology at Manitoba, and later President both there and at Queen's University, Kingston, Canada; Sutherland Simpson, Professor of Physiology, Cornell; James Gunn, Professor of Pharmacology, Oxford, and Director of the Nuffield Institute; John Gunn, Professor of Pharmacology, Cape Town; John Oman, Principal of Westminster (Presbyterian) College, Cambridge; Sir John S. Flett, Director of Geological Survey; Ernest Shearer, Principal of Edinburgh and East of Scotland College of Agriculture – an impressive roll call from a few green Atlantic islands.

Another of Dr McEwen's pupils was the poet Edwin Muir who – he tells us in his *Autobiography* – was afraid of him. Possibly poets were not so well catered for.

Every island and every parish has a large proportion of intelligent countrymen who, through diffidence or poverty, left off their formal education at fourteen. Some of them are as widely read as any professor, with questing omnivorous minds. One of these self-taught scholars was Peter Leith of Appiehouse, on the parish of Stenness. Every Wednesday afternoon you would meet him cycling home from the Public Library in Stromness with a bag of books over his shoulder. You had to climb up a ladder into his book-stacked loft. No man knew more about the curious by-ways of Orkney history and Orkney character than that gentle silken-voiced farmer. From his reservoir of knowledge he left only a few published papers that he had read to the Orkney Antiquarian Society, some newspaper and magazine articles, a brief history of the church in Stenness.

Another was Robert Rendall, a draper in Kirkwall, who taught himself to be a world-acknowledged expert on shells and the life of the shore, and in the latter part of his life wrote marvellous lyrics, some of them as good as anything that has been published in Scotland this century.

There was John Mooney, another Kirkwall businessman of small formal education, author of *Eynhallow, the Holy Island*; *Saint Magnus, Earl of Orkney*; and *The Cathedral and Royal Burgh of Kirkwall*.

One crofter-composer would leave his plough in the half-done furrow when a fragment of a new tune came to him. His wife despaired while his field for the rest of that spring morning was saturated with fiddle music.

There was John Firth, a Finstown joiner, who mastered the plain style of prose and wrote a great book called *Reminiscences of An Orkney Parish*, about the agricultural cycle and parish communal life in the nineteenth century. Labour in the fields was seen as a ritual, a ceremony, a dance of bread.

John Shearer, a former Orkney Director of Education, used to tell his Stromness pupils about a contemporary of his, a Birsay boy called Charles Ballantyne, who went to Kirkwall for his secondary education. He was a brilliant pupil, unsurpassed in every subject in the curriculum, a kind of Admirable Crichton. He was killed in France in the First World War.

The weather is good, if you like a temperate climate. Thermometer and barometer measure our seasons capriciously; the Orkney year should be seen rather as a stark drama of light and darkness. In June and July, at midnight the north is always red; the sun is just under the horizon;

dawn mingles its fires with sunset. In midwinter the sun intrudes for only a few hours into the great darkness, but the January nights are magnificent – star-hung skies, the slow heavy swirling silk of the aurora borealis, the moon in a hundred waters: a silver plate, a broken honeycomb, a cluster of fireflies.

There can be spells of rough weather at all times of the year. Sometimes, winter or summer, the wind breaks bounds and flattens everything. In the great hurricane of January 1952 hen-houses were blown out to sea, cockerels raging aloft over the crested Sounds. A fishing disaster happened last century, in June – a sudden gale that caught the herring fleet off Hoy and swamped two boats.

Rain falls at all seasons, but not so persistently as in the Hebrides or the west of Ireland. A city shower is a meaningless nuisance, a liquidity seeping into collar and trouser-leg. In the north, on a showery day, you can *see* the rain, its lovely behaviour over an island – while you stand a mile off in a patch of sun – Jock's cows in the meadow a huddle of ghosts, Tammy's oat-field jewelled; the clouds a rout of fabulous creatures dissolving at last through their prism . . . Nothing is more lovely than the islands in a shifting dapple of sun and rain.

The wind is rarely still. It shifts from airt to airt, and everything – flowers, clouds, birds, animals, boats – are caught up in the invisible stream. In late summer afternoons the wind goes through the corn in deep resonant surges, but the evenings are marvellously tranquil, except for a broken thunder all along the west coast of Orkney – Noup, The Brough, Marwick, Yesnaby, Black Craig, Rora; the Atlantic glutting itself among the caves and rock-stacks. The sea remembers, like an ancient harp.

In the course of a single day you can see, in that immensity of sky, the dance of sun, cloud, sea-mist, thunder, rain: the endless ballet of the weather.

Everywhere in Orkney there is the sense of age, the dark backward and abysm. The islands have been inhabited for a very long time, from before the day of the plough.

The Norsemen came 1,200 years ago to a place that was already populous with fishermen, herdsmen, farmers; a clever ingenious folk who built 'brochs' along sea coasts and lochs to defend themselves against sea-raiders, or perhaps to dominate a subject population. These primitive castles presented a high blank circular wall to any besiegers. In the open courtyard inside the broch were wells, quernstones, stores of fish and cheese and grain, animals, people able to withstand a long siege. Between the double walls a stone stairway, with galleries, led to the top, from where the defenders could pour savage fire and stone on the enemy below.

But the broch-builders were themselves invaders. The silent vanished races stretch back beyond them, laid in barrows and howes under the green waves of time. Not a spring, but a plough somewhere, turns up another relic.

The first Orkney peoples can only be seen darkly, a few figures on a moorland against the sky, between twilight and night. They are beyond the reach of legend even. Archaeologists describe a Mediterranean folk who committed themselves to the sea. They steered their boats through the Straits and northwards, keeping close inland (for they could not trust such frail vessels far out, with their precious cargo of tribal symbols and secrets, stock, seed, nubile girls), all the way up the coastline of Spain and France. Instinctively, like all voyagers, they veered west, until they rounded the Scillies. Still they sailed north into the widening light – they would have planned their journey for the summer – past Wales and Man, the southern coast of Scotland, the many Hebrides. Beyond the savage bulk of Cape Wrath there was empty ocean, until in a summer dawn they saw the Orkneys like sleeping whales. There they made landfall. It seemed a likely place, secure from whatever dynastic tyranny or famine or plague or population pressure they had fled from. The sounds and seas about the islands swarmed with fish, the hills with birds and hares. They hauled their boats into the shelter of Rackwick, Yesnaby, Skaill, Aikerness.

Hardly a thing is known about these first Orkneymen (if they were the first Orkneymen) apart from the monuments they left behind them, the huge stones of Maeshowe and Brodgar, and the pastoral village of Skara Brae in the west. History can tell nothing; not a word or a name comes out of the silence – there are a few ambiguous scratches on a wall at Skara Brae. We wander clueless through immense tracts of time. Imagination stirs about a scattered string of bone beads found in Skara Brae. Did the girl have no time for adornment when a westerly gale choked the doors with sand; or did sea raiders tear them from her neck? . . . The Skara Brae dwellers had lost the skills and mysteries of agriculture; they were shepherds and fishermen of a primitive kind. The sand sifted through doors and roofs, and soon their village was a blank; until another nineteenth-century gale laid bare an arrangement of stones.

The Orkney imagination is haunted by time; it is Edwin Muir's great theme, and in this matter he is the poet who speaks for all of us. Critics wonder at the heraldic imagery of his poetry.

> Long since we were a family, a people,
> The legends say; an old kind-hearted king
> Was our foster-father, and our life a fable.
>
> Nature in wrath broke through the grassy ring
> Where all our gathered treasures lay in sleep –
> Many a rich and many a childish thing.
>
> She filled with hoofs and horns the quiet keep.
> Her herds beat down the turf and nosed the shrine
> In bestial wonder, bull and adder and ape,

Lion and fox, all dressed by fancy fine
In human flesh and armed with arrows and spears;
But on the brow of each a secret sign . . .

What fed Edwin Muir's heart and mind with such archaic
pellucid imagery? There were withered sandstone emblems
over the lairds' and merchants' gates. But I think it is more the
look of the islands that suggests heraldic stillness and a hoarded
symbolism – quarterings on the hill, pasture and meadow and
cornfield, a slow change throughout the year; and, older
still, the great shield of the sky swarming with azure and gule,
and clouds like fabulous beasts rampant.

Heraldry is the mysterious signs, deeper than art or language, by which a family or a tribe pass on their most precious
secrets, their lore of a kingdom lost. It is a stillness into which
the torrents of history are gathered, like an unflawed mill
pool. In the silence an image out of the past stirs, and illumin-
ates things in our present circumstances, as individuals or as
citizens of a country or as members of the human race, that
we do not understand. Heraldry is the fury of history made
wise and formal; from its hands we take at last the wholesome
images – the heart's bread – that our ancestors sowed for us in
passion and blindness. That quiet pool turns the millstones
of religion, and of art, and of the simple graces and courtesies
of daily living.

It is impossible to understand Orkney in any prosaic way,
as many people try to do, by reading tables of statistics about
egg production or population drift, concerned only with the
here and the now. Contemporary Orkney, cut off from the
story of its past, is meaningless. The majority of Orcadians
have a kind of reverence for their history, but it is a romantic
reverence, for the witches, the press-gang, the smugglers,
the salt-tongued ministers, the Hudson's Bay men, and above
all for the Vikings; a kind of sentimental make-believe history,
very different from the terrible and fruitful things that

actually happened to our ancestors.

For the Vikings especially we keep a welcome; they are our true ancestors who came by the salt road, west-over-sea from Norway, a thousand years ago and more; we are blood of their blood, a pure stock. (Such myths, in Germany only a few years ago, produced the greatest nightmare in history.) If the Viking myth is true, it is true with so many reservations and qualifications as to be almost meaningless. No harm is done, except that the corridors of history get filled with unreal figures and hollow voices, and so we ourselves become part of a phantasmagoria. In this book an attempt is made to see the Vikings plain.

I often think we are not really interested in the past at all. There is a new religion, Progress, in which we all devoutly believe, and it is concerned only with material things in the present and in a vague golden-handed future. It is a rootless utilitarian faith, without beauty or mystery; a kind of blind unquestioning belief that men and their material circumstances will go on improving until some kind of nirvana is reached and everyone will be rich, free, fulfilled, well-informed, masterful. Why should Orcadians not believe in Progress? – everything seems to insist on it. The stone cots of their grandfathers, where men and animals bedded down under the same roof, are strewn all about the parishes and islands, beside the smart modern houses of wood and concrete. The horses are banished, but then tractors and lorries are much less trouble, much more efficient. There is no real poverty any more; tramps and vagrants and tinkers are exiled with the horses. (Only the very backward farmers nowadays don't have a car.) Progress is a goddess who, up to now, has looked after her children well. The sky is scored with television aerials. There is a family planning centre. There are drifts of books and oil paintings and gramophone records everywhere. And still the shower of good things intensifies.

It is difficult to picture this goddess of plenty other than as some huge computer-figure, that will give our children what they desire easily and endlessly – food, sex, excitement – a synthetic goddess, vast and bland as Buddha, but without love or tenderness or compassion; activated only by a mania to create secondary objects that become increasingly shinier and shoddier and uglier.

I feel that this religion is in great part a delusion, and will peter out in the marsh. A community like Orkney dare not cut itself off from its roots and sources. Places like Rackwick and Eynhallow have no meaning if you try to describe or evaluate them in terms of a newspaper article. They cannot be described in that way.

The goddess exacts tribute in subtle ways. For example: there is a kind of shame nowadays in using the old words. And Orkney, only a generation ago, abounded in characters, surrealist folk walked our roads and streets, Dickensian figures with earth and salt in them. Nowadays there is a distinct trimming and levelling-up; a man is ashamed to be different from his neighbour. The old stories have vanished with the horses and the tinkers; instead of the yarn at the pier-head or the pub, you are increasingly troubled with bores who insist on telling you what they think about Viet Nam or the bank rate or heart transplants, and you may be sure it isn't their own thought-out opinion at all, but some discussion they have heard on TV the night before, or read in the *Daily Express* – and now, having chewed it over, they must regurgitate it for you.

Word and name are drained of their ancient power. Number, statistic, graph are everything.

We have come a long way in a few years.

It is a word, blossoming as legend, poem, story, secret, that holds a community together and gives a meaning to its life. If words become functional ciphers merely, as they are in white papers and business letters, they lose their 'ghosts' – the rich aura that has grown about them from the start, and grows infinitesimally richer every time they are spoken. They lose more; they lose their 'kernel', the sheer sensuous relish of utterance. Poetry is a fine interpretation of ghost and kernel. We are in danger of contenting ourselves with husks. For example, nowadays we say 'it rains'. The old Orkneymen had a range of words for every kind and intensity of rain – a driv, a rug, a murr, a hagger, a dagg, a rav, a hellyiefer. This is a measure of how our feeling for language has coarsened in a generation or two. The same trend is noticeable when a modern islander builds a house; more likely than not he will call it something insipid and meaningless, like 'Sunnybrae' or 'Roseville'. The names of the old farms are functional, powerful, beautiful – Skaill, Quoyostray, Lyking, Stymilders, Breckness, Corse, Tormiston.

Newspapers erode the language with their daily poundings. A lighthouse-keeper breaks his leg, say, on a skerry, and is taken by helicopter to hospital. MERCY FLIGHT says the headline next morning in *The Press and Journal*. The word 'mercy' is drained of its ancient hallowed meaning; we can never know whether the helicopter pilot and those who despatched him and those who receive the sufferer feel any mercy; we must hope that they do; the only sure thing is that the divine quality of mercy is progressively crippled by wrong usage – as if a great angel had been shorn of its wings.

The attitude of a people to death, and the language they use about it, is always significant. 'Many a proud lady, low stooping, has entered here,' wrote a Norseman with his axe on the wall of Maeshowe, looking at the slender skull and bones in the burial cavity. The old fisherman in Robert Rendall's poem died 'e'en as a cruisie (lamp) flickers oot, unslockt' (unquenched). 'I will not be going home today,' says Thorstein, the young Icelander, tying his shoe-string on the battlefield of Clontarf, the army in ruin and flight all about him – 'I will not be going home today, I live out in Iceland.' ... This gaiety in face of the last and greatest enemy has fallen to the ludicrous rhymes of the *In Memoriam* column.

Decay of language is always the symptom of a more serious sickness.

In the following chapters in this book I am not going to dwell on Orkney's progress in a few years out of serfdom into full economic freedom; the symbols of that emergence lie thick everywhere in the islands. The forward-looking Orkney has been dealt with elsewhere.

I will attempt to get back to the roots and sources of the community, from which it draws its continuing life, from which it cuts itself off at its peril. With the help of the old stories, the old scrolls, the gathered legends, and the individual earth-rooted imagination, I will try to discover a line or two of the ancient life-giving heraldry.

2

RACKWICK

RACKWICK

THE ISLAND of Hoy (Haey, 'the high island', to the first Norse settlers) is heaped up massively at its northern and central parts with dark rounded hills. To the south there is a fine harbour and prosperous farms. Facing Scapa Flow is Lyness, like a Yukon shanty town abandoned after a gold rush. In two world wars this ugly settlement flourished, with navvies and sailors in the streets and canteens and stores, and the ships of the Royal Navy coming and going in Scapa Flow. Now Lyness rots, unlamented. There is a fringe of tilth and pasture in the north of Hoy, along the shore: the road goes this far. Another road branches westward between the hills, into utter desolation, a place of kestrels and peatbogs. One thinks of the psalmist and his vale of death. After five miles the road ends abruptly at a glint of sea and the farm of Glen. The dark hills are still all round, but they hold in their scarred hands a green valley. This is Rackwick. The bowl is tilted seawards – its lip is a curving bay, half huge round sea-sculptured boulders, half sand. Out in the bay, like guardians, stand two huge cliffs, The Sneuk and The Too.

A burn, having gathered its waters from the surrounding

hills, fed with small tinkling tributaries, moves slowly through the valley; it deepens into a reflective pool; then rushes foaming at the sea over a ravelment of round boulders. After a heavy rainfall the stepping-stones are awash.

The poignant thing about this beautiful valley ('the bay of wreckage') is that, apart from Glen, farmed by Jack Rendall, it has been utterly abandoned. The floor of the valley and its fertile western slope are littered with half-ruined crofts – the windows blind, the roofs fallen in, the hearth-stones forever black. Here and there among the barns and outhouses are stone jars, rusted ploughs, broken cups. There was abundant life in Rackwick once; the life ebbed out rapidly through some flaw; the place is full of the ghosts of centuries.

The first longship, having probed among the north islands – Rinansay, Sanday, Stronsay, Rousay – and seen the farms of new settlers everywhere, steered into the open ocean and turned south along the coast of the large island called Hrossey ('the horse island'). The line of crags was broken here and there by bays, Marwick, Skaill, Yesnaby; there was a boat on every beach and a new farm steading above the curve of the bay. The longship, with its plough and bag of seed corn, sailed south in growing darkness. Hamnavoe was a cluster of lanterns. The crags of Hoy at first light towered above them, pillars of fire. Towards noon they came to Rackwick.

> Beach shineth in blackness,
> After hard voyage a hidden valley,
> Hills for bees to be hived,
> Beasts kept, a cod-hungry boat,
> A comfort of fire in the crofts.
> We furled sail, set firm our feet,
> Stone laid against stone,
> Laboured long till ebb of light,

Hungry men round a dead hearth.
Dreamed I that darkness
Of horse, harp, a hallowed harvest.

The first crofts were hacked and dug and drained from obdurate virgin soil above the shore. Hard to tell what starved sick months passed, fed with limpets and crabs, till the first corn came and grew and yellowed, a thin harvest. They cut querns from the round stones on the beach. In winter they ate shellfish till their guts loathed them. Three old people died. Thorkeld went after gulls' eggs in the crag and never came home. Ubi found a way of snaring rabbits. The children were thin and querulous as birds. The people could not have survived that first winter and spring if they had not been driven by some harsh will; who fixed yokes on the shoulders of the women, and plucked a hawk from the hill and hooded it, and directed the gathering of stones for dwellings and barns, and set a man on guard over a bag of sacred corn, and gave a good ration to the fishermen and breeding women, and let the old sick folk die in silence. They could not have survived but for that leader who was half a god and half a beast.

The second harvest was good.

In spring they drained and dug new fields from the western slope. Everybody, even the children and the old people, gathered stones for the long hall of their chief. Twice or thrice a year the chief went to the assembly of chiefs, the 'Thing', in the Island of Horses. A Celtic priest would stay for a night in the chief's house. He told the chief that the people must build a chapel for the offering of Mass and the greater glory of God. The chief considered that his hall should be extended, with a room for guests and a room where brides should lie with him first, before they went to their husbands, and a storehouse for ale. But in the end the chapel was built. The Abbot of Eynhallow came and blessed the chapel, flinging holy water about him, and said the first Mass.

Frik, who was the best stoneworker in the valley, found a long blue stone in the ebb. He squared one end of the stone so that it stood upright. He carved with chisel and hammer dove eyes in the stone. He carried Our Lady of Rackwick into the chapel. That night the statue of Our Lady stood in a corner of the chapel, her feet dappled with seven candle flames. Next morning she was placed in the open air, on the hill, between fields and sea; it seemed her dove eyes kept watch over the labours of fishermen and ploughmen, Our Lady of Furrows.

In spring there was ploughing again. The one black ox was yoked, the large field round the Hall was ploughed before the small rigs on the western hill slope. After the sowing, the valley people saw the longships from more prosperous islands sailing west through the Pentland Firth on the spring cruise. The crofters and shepherds of Orkney were pirates for the rest of the summer. But the chief had no longship; the valley was too poor to go a-Viking. The best they could manage was a foray in darkness across the Pentland Firth to get Caithness sheep.

In the month of May they dug peats from the moor. The peats for the Hall fires were dug and wind-dried and stacked before the peasants took their own peats home.

On a fine morning they became fishermen. They slowly charted in their memories the outswirls and currents of the Pentland Firth. They learned to fish further and further out. They set lobster creels under the Atlantic cliff-line. (The chief's men carried all the best fish to the kitchen in the Hall.) They learned to read this new sky for storms. When the firth was stormy and the fishing boats out the valley women would turn to the statue in the hills.

Our Lady of the Boat
Our Lady of Oil and Salt

Our Lady of the Inshore
Our Lady of the Silver Dancers
Our Lady of Nets
Our Lady of the Atlantic
Star of the Sea
   May cuithe and codling hang in
      the peatsmoke.

But still it sometimes happened that a boat would not return.

Twice or thrice a year a priest would come and say a Mass in the chapel. He would baptise the infants, anoint the old sick people, marry those who were troubled with the fires of lust. Afterwards he would read the gospel to them, the miracles and parables, and how Christ loved the poor more than the rich. The chief got red in the face and shifted in his seat whenever the priest said that. But into the crofter's sackcloth the life of Christ wove richness and beauty.

The mason made Stations of the Cross for the chapel, putting blue and red clay and egg-yolk among the shallow scratchings of fourteen stones, so that the passion of Christ along three walls of the church was like the year-long labour of a crofter from furrow to loaf-and-ale. The cross a ploughshare; Veronica a croft girl risen in pity from her spinning wheel; lance and sword the harvest sickles; the flagellating flails, the grinding millstones and black oxen of execution; the last stone, tabernacle of birth and death and resurrection – from it issues for ever the Bread of Heaven.

Condemnation
The winter jar of honey and grain
Is a Lenten urn.

Cross
Lord, it is time. Take our yoke
And sunwards turn.

First Fall
To drudge in furrows till you drop
Is to be born.

Mother of God
Out of the mild mothering hill
And the chaste burn.

Simon
God-begun, the barley rack
By man is borne.

Veronica
Foldings of women. Your harrow sweat
Darkens her yarn.

Second Fall
Sower-and-Seed, one flesh, you fling
From stone to thorn.

Women of Jerusalem
You are bound for the Kingdom of Death. The enfolded
Women mourn.

Third Fall
Scythes are sharpened to bring you down,
King Barleycorn.

The Stripping
Flails creak. Golden coat
From kernel is torn.

The Crucifixion
The fruitful stones thunder around,
Quern on quern.

Death
The last black hunger rages through you
With hoof and horn.

Pieta
Mother, fold him from those furrows,
Your broken bairn.

Sepulchre
Shepherd, angel, king are kneeling, look,
In the door of the barn.

In the late summer they saw the Viking ships sailing back
through the Pentland Firth. They took their sickles to the big
field round the Hall. It was good weather for fishing but the
boats were hauled on the beach. Rain or wind might tangle
the stalks; the chief's harvest must be cut while the burnish
was on it. Then, wind or rain or sun, the crofters could turn
to their own yellow strips.

At the Harvest Home the men all got drunk, as if the winter
would be a long holiday. A few women, thinking of the
labour still to be done, lingered round the statue in the hills.

> Our Lady of Cornstalks
> Our Lady of the Flail
> Our Lady of Winnowing
> Our Lady of Quernstones
> Our Lady of the Oven
> Blue Tabernacle
> Our Lady of the Five Loaves
>   Take the ploughman home from
>   the ale-house sober.

The best butter and honeycombs and the first sacks of meal
and malt were carried into the chief's storehouse.

The chief was a busy man all winter. He drew plans, made
calculations, on bits of parchment. This piece of the hill
Moorfea would be ploughed out in February; another fishing
boat – broader, longer, heavier – must be built, one that
could venture into the Atlantic. Three girls were ready for
marriage, they would be disposed on this crofter and that

fisherman and the other shepherd, with full acknowledgement on the part of all concerned that the *ius primae noctis* would be observed in favour of the chief. If his own rental reached a certain figure, then his voice would carry more weight at the assembly of chiefs, the 'Thing'. If he saved hard enough, he might manage to make a Viking cruise himself some summer, in partnership with the minor chiefs in Voes and Hoy, one longship between the three of them. His Hall would be the better of some English tapestries, Irish silver, French wine jars. His name might even be mentioned in a poem or a saga. It was a great nuisance having to provide for the maintenance of clergy – the priests were supposed to be espoused to poverty, and there was the Abbot living as grandly as the Earl himself – he would raise that matter at the next Thing (not that the voice of a poor chief like him was likely to be listened to).

The chief drank a great quantity of ale-and-honey on winter nights, and ate salted mutton, and ate smoked fish on Friday. The peasants ate smoked fish every day of the week, and by the beginning of Lent their ale was sour. They went out to plough with hollow bellies.

The two shepherds had a busy time in March. The ewes dropped their lambs quickly, at all hours of the day and night, a few dead but most of them sound and healthy, and here and there twins. One lamb was born under the statue in the hills, while all round the crofters were putting torches to the dry heather, small red flickers among drifts of grey smoke: the muirburn.

> Our Lady of Lent
> Our Lady of the Last Snow
> Our Lady of Muirburn
> Fold of the Agnus Dei
> Our Lady of Quiet Waters
> Our Lady of Daffodils

Our Lady of April
Guard the labour of thirty
five ewes.

Then they saw a small grey cowled figure come walking
between the hills. It was the priest, carrying the box of cinders
for Ash Wednesday.

The people of the valley knelt side by side in the church,
the chief who didn't like the idea of death shoulder to shoulder
with old Sig, who was twisted with all kinds of pain and said
she wished she were in two places at the one time, in the
kirkyard and in heaven. The priest put ashes on the foreheads
of everyone to remind them that they were dust and would
return to dust. Then he preached a sermon.

The plough has broken the lingering snow.
Fields are seeded and harrowed.
Tar is bright
On the net, the oar, the stone, the shed.
But only a few sour fish
Smoked over peats
Lie between the crust and the last ale
And thin hands droop round the table.
Days are dreicher than January.
A dead lamb is dropped in the thaw.
Yet now we are glad
For all things turn to the sun.
Our hands reach across light to shoal and sheaf.
A lamb flutters across the hill.
We are glad, we give thanks
That the Christ of loaves and fishes shared our labour,
His hammer beat ploughs,
He hauled a loaded net from the outswirls of ebb.
The girls and widows
Magnify God with Mary in the coldness of March.
(Now lambs come fast in the lee of the dyke.)

We fishermen, crofters, women give thanks
For now the Child roots in the womb of his Mother,
All summer and autumn harbours there,
And poor and white
Will open omnipotent eyes to a dazzle of snow.
In this grey hungry time between plough and quernstones,
We praise thee, Lord of Lent,
For all the year's brightness, snow and lamb and bread.

Life went on that way for centuries in Rackwick. Birth, love, labour, death – this was the rhythm of the crofter-fisherman's life, generation after generation. They spoke the Norn language that the first settlers had brought over the sea from Norway.

One winter their chief died and there was no son to follow him; only three white-handed daughters that he had married off among the islands, to substantial traders and farmers. The windows of the Hall were shuttered, locks rusted in the doors. The crofters began to think, as the months passed, that their days of tax-paying were over. They gathered their fleeces and cut their corn eagerly the next August.

Seven scythes leaned at the wall.
Beard upon golden beard
The last barley loaded
Swayed through the yard.
The girls uncorked the ale.
Fiddle and feet moved together.
Then between stubble and heather
A horseman rode.

The horseman had ridden from Hoy; he spoke a hard foreign language that they hardly understood, but they did manage to take in that he was the new chief's factor; that their chief was now chief of the whole island, and lived in a large new Hall on the other side of the hills; that their chief was a Scotsman and called himself 'laird'; and that their rents were substantially increased as from the Martinmas term.

Mucklehouse, a barrel of butter, salted. *The Shore*, a barrel of herring, salted. *Burnmouth*, seven load of building stones from the ebb. *Ootrow*, malt, a hundredweight. *Quernstones*, barley, a hundredweight, ground. *Bunertoon*, a young goat. *Scar*, a thatch for kirk and Hall. *Midhouse*, three round straw baskets, plaited, yellow as June suns. *North-house*, a provision of winter fiddle music, at the Hall, as often as called on. *Crowsnest*, a hawk from the hill, unhooded. *Moss*, a stack of peats for Hall and Manse. *Greenhill*, seven wet cheeses, white as winter suns. *Reumin*, sea timber for the new pews. *Glen*, three sides of pork, salted . . . And forbye they maun labour, ilk ane, in the laird his oat field and barley field, until sic time as the hairst, so may it please God, be gaitherit in.

About that time a terrible thing happened. A dozen horsemen rode through the hills from Hoy. They dismounted at the chapel of Our Lady. The valley people heard the sounds of blows and smashing and dilapidation inside – it went on all morning. Presently some of the horsemen came out with bulging sacks and staggered with their loads to the edge of the crag and emptied them out into the sea below. A young man with a pale face stood at the end of the chapel and told the people that now they could worship God in a pure form; the Pope and his bishops had been cast down from their high Babylonish places; the idolatry of the Mass was abolished, abomination of desolation that it was; instead the unadulterated word would be preached to them, Sabbath after Sabbath, by him their new minister, in the kirk of Hoy five miles away. And had any illegitimate bairns been born in Hoy that past summer? Thomas Manson and Sarah Corrigall, standing at the fringe of the crowd, hung their heads. Thomas Manson was summoned to do public penance in the kirk of Hoy on Sabbath first.

> Thomas Manson, fornicator, thou art here upstood
> For that at harvest, behind a stook
> In the time of ale, fiddles, and dancing,
> Or in a beached boat, at Burnmouth,
> When the basket of fish was divided
> And the women took twine to a torn net,
> Or on Kringnafea, one day of fleeces
> – Whiter thou and she
> Than the wanton innocent shivering beasts
>
> There or elsewhere in the country of love
>
> Thou debauched Sarah Corrigall, spinster.
> In Rackwick that winter
> An untimely cradle was hammered.
> Stand therefore, Thomas Manson,
> Three sequent Sabbaths, in sackcloth,
> Before the elect.
> Purge thy lust with public confession.
> (The ninth moon will chasten Sarah.)
> In that flame stand the holy cup and bread.

When the strangers had ridden off the Rackwick folk peered through the door of their chapel. The strangers had made it starker than any stable. The sanctuary light was out. Altar, tabernacle, crucifix, the statue of Saint Magnus, the Stations of the Cross, were torn down. Their treasures were taken from them. They turned for home, poor people indeed.

Everything was utterly changed. The chief who, in spite of everything, had been their protector, was a stranger now and an extortioner. The religion that had sweetened their labours and sufferings was a creed now of terror and hellfire. Our Lady of Furrows on the side of the hill was left to them; but she had to be visited secretly, at night, for even in the

valley were one or two folk who whispered at the side door
of manse or Hall, and winked and pointed fingers, and were
closeted for an hour at a time with the Aberdeenshire factor . . . Their green peace was broken. Horsemen rode
through the hills at all seasons. Everywhere was a pointing
of fingers. Words were uttered that they could not understand – for example, Witch.

Three horsemen rode between the hills
And they dismounted at Greenhill
Tall they stooped in at the door.
No long time then
Till Wilma came out among them, laughing.
The bible fishermen watched from the shore.
She sat behind the second dark rider.
They left the valley at noon.
And Wilma did not come back that day
Nor the next day
Nor any day at all that week.
And the dog barked lonely at Greenhill
And the girls took turns at milking her cow
(One took the froth from her vat.)
The laird sent word
At the end of winter, to James of Reumin
That on Candlemas Friday
He should sail his dinghy to Kirkwall.
He sailed the *Lupin* to the red church.
And there at a steep place, Gallowsha,
Among tilted bottles, fists, faces
– A cold drunken wheel –
James saw the hangman put the red shirt on Wilma.
He sailed back smouldering
From the fire, the rum, the reproaches.
The dog of Greenhill
Barked in the throat of the valley.

And next morning
They launched their boat at the dawn with a wild shout,
The twelve unlucky fishermen.

Sometimes the horsemen would carry off a young man for
His Majesty's ships of war, and leave a guinea on the table,
bounty money. As the wars against the French dragged on,
more and more valley men were impressed. The women
complained long and bitterly to the laird. But the laird could
do nothing; he himself was under compulsion.

I, Harry Cruickshank, laird in Hoy
Being by your lordships bidden
To supply from my lands in Rackwick, Hoy
For His Majesty's ships-of-war
Seven hale hearty willing seamen
Upon payment of the agreed bounty, two guineas,
Did thereupon name

John Stewart at Greenhill, fisherman,
James Stewart at Greenhill, crofter,
William Mowat, at Bunertoon, fisherman,
Andrew Sinclair at Mucklehouse, fisherman,
Thomas Thomson at Crowsnest, fisherman,
James Robb at Scar, fisherman,
James Leask at Reumin, crofter and fisherman.
All unmarried, save for William Mowat
Who got wife and cow from Graemsay at the fall of the year
And James Robb, a widower –
The rest all young men in their strength.
I duly rode with officers to the valley
To give notice of impressment to the said men
But found them removed
And the old people dumb and cold as stones.
One said, they were gone fishing, very far out –
Faroe, Rockall, Sulisker.

Another, to the horse market in Caithness.
Another, 'the trows wur taen them aneath the hill . . .'
Upon the Sabbath following
I came to the kirk of Hoy secretly with four officers
Between the sermon and the last psalm.
We took John and James Stewart in the kirk door.
They were quiet enough after the minister spoke with them.
(By this, they will be in Portsmouth.)
It is certain, my lords,
Robb and Thomson are in the caves.
Andrew Sinclair, fisherman, Mucklehouse,
Listed in Hamnavoe for the Davis Straits
On the whaler *Tavistock*
(We found his mark and name in the agent's book)
And Mowat ferried himself to Graemsay
With wife and cow
And there hacked three fingers from his right hand
And stifled the ruin with tar.
As for Leask, he is broken with troll-music.
He lies day-long in the back of the bed,
Dark hollows about his skull.
The old woman says, 'in a decline, consumption'.
She stitches away at a shroud.
But like enough, the guns being silent
And Buonaparte down,
He will make his customary furrows along the hill.
A dozen old men are left in the valley.
Last week, your lordships,
I observed two women rowing to the lobsters.
Ploughmen next April will have shrill voices.

When Queen Victoria came to the throne (the factor
brought the news to them; for the laird occasionally got
The Times newspaper from London and *The Scotsman* news-

paper from Edinburgh, whenever a sailing packet arrived at Hamnavoe from Leith) there came a time of peace to the people of the valley. The whole nation seemed to burgeon; procreation was all; the Queen herself set an example. The very hens in those years had larger broods. In this remote valley, too, there were more children than the fields could hold. The young men went whaling to the Davis Strait, they worked for the fur traders in Hudson's Bay, they became seamen in the British merchant service. Even the Orkneymen who remained were powered by this huge Victorian energy.

'Once he disputed
The Kame with an eagle,
His two lambs
Fluttering on a sea ledge . . .

'That storm in '75
When *Swift* and *Dolphin* drowned
He beached in Lewis
Up to the thwart in haddocks . . .

'In jail twice
For drunk fighting . . .

'Twelve bairns called him da
In Flotta and Hoy.
Three sat at his lawful table . . .

'And he broke six rocks
Before his plough
Stitched on the bog and heather and stone of Moorfea
One green square . . .

'He was at the whaling a winter . . .

'An old silver man
He reads his bible now
And yawns a bit'.

The impression has perhaps been given in this chapter of a simple pastoral community hardly touched by the Fall; but evil is universal, and the simpler the society the starker it appears. In the interests of truth it is time to weave a dark thread into the tapestry. The Rackwick men, in common with other Orcadians and islanders all over the world, were wreckers – that is, from earliest times they plundered ships that went ashore, and sometimes they did so with a terrible ferocity. This lawless activity had the sanction of custom, and sometimes even of authority. One eighteenth-century island minister is said to have prayed in his pulpit, 'O Lord, if it is thy will to cause ships to go ashore, dinna forget the poor island of Sanday . . .' In some places lanterns were lit among the rocks so that merchant ships would be confused in the darkness and founder on the crags, and it is probable that the Rackwick men did this too. They were favoured in that they lived on the most treacherous coast in Europe, abrupt huge crags – dark angels, widow-makers – stretching away on each side of the valley, and the fierce weavings of the Pentland Firth between them and Scotland. The nineteenth-century journalist J. R. Tudor records one incident of many: 'Peterkin narrates how the good ship *Albion*, of Blyth, was, in November, 1815, driven ashore at a place called the Stower, between the Old Man and Roray Head (337 feet). Only two of the crew were left on the ill-fated craft, all the rest had been washed overboard. Of the two survivors one was lashed to the rigging, the other was lying insensible on the deck. Such was the state of things, when some fishermen from Rackwick, clambering down through a cleft in the rocks, boarded the vessel and proceeded, as was the custom in those days, to plunder the cargo. Having done so, they carried the man who had been lying on the deck, ashore, and left him on a shelf of the cliff, still alive, "all night – a night of November, when the earth was buried in deep snow, when an intense frost prevailed, and when a piercing sea-wind would have chilled to death, on the rocks of Hoy, the most vigorous human being, if opposed in a state of inaction to its power". That these savages could easily have removed the man to the summit of the cliffs, and thence to shelter, was proved by their dragging up a companion, who had got drunk on the rum they had found on board. The next day the unfortunate seaman was found dead, as also his messmate who had been made fast to the rigging, and who the wreckers, in their hurry to plunder, had overlooked. Peterkin states both of these unfortunates were buried on the spot . . .'

Is there any excuse for such barbarity? One may whisper, in part mitigation, that their lives were stark and uncertain; they saw cruelty as a necessary part of the pattern of all existence. Their winters were generally hungry, and a broken cargo on the rocks was a windfall from the uncertain hands of Fate. (Fate had ruled the lives of the first settlers. The predestination that after centuries of catechism and kirk discourse was now a part of their outlook is only a more sophisticated name for that fate, and certainly one reason why they felt at home with Calvinism, in spite of everything.)

And the sea must have her own. For them the sea was a being of enormous power, a goddess, a provider and a destroyer. They had to live on intimate terms with the sea, unblessed now, whether they wanted to or not. It put the grey colour in their eyes, their voices were modulated to its sounds and silences. The sea, unblessed now since heather had grown over the long stone on the hill, gave them fish, seaweed, salt, driftwood, seals, birds. They were the children of the unblessed sea. This capricious mother had her rights; especially she claimed as her own the bodies of men who had hazarded themselves in boats, put themselves in her care. If she chose to take a few of these children to herself – even the best mother is capricious and this one was unblessed – then it would be highly dangerous, to say the least, for her other children to attempt any kind of rescue, life-saving, resuscitation. A drowning hand was allowed to slip from the rock into the suck, the drench, the silence.

Wreckers, fishermen, shepherds, crofters, their lives remained hard. The burden of watching and waiting remained, as always, with the women. Now Our Lady of Furrows was no longer there to help the women in their long vigils. The stone with dove eyes had long since fallen and been woven over with heather. Girls and wives and widows watched alone, in stormy nightfalls when the fishing boats were still at sea, folding about them in the darkness griefs more ancient than agriculture.

What they fold, what the shepherds fold
Is this, in March,
A mothering flock.

The crofter's trade a hoarding, folding, flowering,
Of seed from snow.
What the fishermen fold is this,
A sklinter of haddocks
From the breached banks of the sea.

What the women fold
Are torn nets, a stretch of yarn from the loom,
Sheaf after sheaf of August oats,
In the cupboard cheese and honey and ale and bread,
Shapes in the womb,
Night long as a shroud when the twelve boats
Are drifting lights in the west,
And the ebb ravels itself in rock and sand.

A winter bride is ravished with plough and seed
And finds at last
The crag where mother and widow enfolded stand.

We may hope that now and then a Rackwick woman,

kneeling in pity over a broken spar or a salted sea-boot, redeemed the valley.

Sometimes a lonely ragged figure wandered from croft to croft, an outcast, asking for a cup of milk or a round of bere bannock. These vagrants were feared because – it was believed – they had the power of the evil eye, they were likely to put a curse on the cornfield or the byre if they didn't get what they wanted. They slept in ditches and quarries and the lee of dykes, they were filthy and half-starved, and they begged in a half-Irish tongue with a kind of sharp dangerous keening in it. They weren't particular about lifting an egg from under a hen or a crab from a creel or a few peats as they passed a stack. But Ikey was free of the peasants' monotonous fecund cycle; his day was filled with a wild shameless gaiety.

A ditch awakening,
A bee in my hair.

Egg and honeycomb,
Cold fare.

An ox on the hill,
Gulls, ploughman, ploughshare.

A sharp wet wind
And my bum bare.

A fish-brimming corn-crammed house,
But a hard door.

Chicken, thief, and crab
Round a blink of fire.

A length of bones in the ditch,
A broken prayer.

Time and chance happened to the valley. Changes came in the way of progress that were considered to be good. A new local newspaper, *The Orcadian*, came, a single copy, and was passed from croft to croft. A young voice read it aloud while everybody sat around the open peat fire. Subtly the notion of progress insinuated itself. This reading of newsprint was thought to be a great advance on the chanting of old winter stories. The iron crusie-lamp, fed with fish oil, a dried reed-pith for wick, went down before the paraffin lamp. It was more convenient to cook on a black 'enchantress' range than over the open hearth fire that never went out from generation to generation. Loaves from the bakehouses of Hamnavoe gradually ousted oatcake and bere bannock: to begin with a slice of white bread was lingered over like cake, and on Sunday mornings as a special treat they had tea instead of milk and ale. A school was built under Moorfea after the Scottish Education Act of 1872. A new wooden shop sold paraffin, tea, biscuits, flour, boots, sweets, twine, sugar. The fishermen gazed in wonderment for the first time on oranges and apples; it is likely that some of the older men resented such novelty.

> No red orchards here. The sea
>   Throbbing, cold root
> To salt incessant blossoming
>   Burdens the net
> With gray and with white and with blue fruit.

One man, the beachcomber, went his teetering way among the rocks after a storm, profiting from the uneasy truce of sea and shore. The valley got its name from the wreckage the beachcomber trafficked in; in this mystical realm where the giving of names seals a place with its destiny, he was the lord of the valley, the original inhabitant, and perhaps the last.

> Monday I found a boot –
> Rust and salt leather.
> I gave it back to the sea, to dance in.

Tuesday a spar of timber worth thirty bob.
Next winter
It will be a chair, a coffin, a bed.

Wednesday I tangled with Ikey the tinker
For a can of Swedish spirit.
Then we got drunk together behind the rock.

Thursday I got nothing, seaweed,
A whale bone,
Wet feet and a loud cough.

Friday I held a seaman's skull,
Sand spilling from it
The way time is told on kirkyard stones.

Saturday a barrel of sodden oranges.
A Spanish ship
Was wrecked last month at The Kame.

Sunday, for fear of the elders,
I sit on my bum.
What's heaven? A sea chest with a thousand gold coins.

In 1888 the Crofters' Commission finally broke the power of the landed gentry and gave the peasants of Scotland a measure of freedom. The Orkney courts, sitting in Stromness and Kirkwall and the North Isles, drastically reduced rents that they considered extortionate and gave the crofters security of tenure. If at any time they moved from their crofts the owner had to compensate them adequately for any improvements they had carried out.

It was the end of the laird's power. Henceforward, impoverished in their large empty houses, they devoted themselves to County Council work, the Volunteers, lifeboat and hospital committees.

Once it was spring with me
   Stone shield and sundial
Lily and lamb in the Lenten grass;
The ribs of crag and tree
   Resurrecting with birds;
In the mouths of passing crofter and fisher lass
Shy folded words.

Then one tall summer came
   Stone shield and sundial
The year of gun and rod and hawk;
The hills all purple flame;
   The burn flashing with trout;
Candle-light, claret, kisses, witty talk,
Crinoline, flute.

Autumn, all russet, fell
   Stone shield and sundial
I wore the golden harvest beard,
I folded my folk well
   Within our fable.
Elders and councillors hung upon my word
At the long table.

Now winter shrinks the heart
   Stone shield and sundial
I'd trade this cold blank heraldry
To drive with Jock in his cart
   To the hill for peat,
Or seed a field, or from clutches of sea
Take a torn net.

The city continued to shower the gifts of progress on the country people – rubber boots, primus stoves, novels, religious tracts, lemonade, Tilley lamps, cloth caps, bicycles, fly papers, cough mixture, marmalade, a hard metalled road between the hills instead of summer dust and winter quagmires. Life had never been easier for them. Just at this point the people began to leave the valley; they wanted to be nearer the source of all this affluence; 'the drift from the isles' had begun.

The notion of progress is not easy to take root in an elemental community; the people are conservative, cling hard to tradition which is their only sure foothold and the ground of all their folk wisdom and art and of the precarious crafts by which they lived. But by the turn of the century everything conspired to nurture the root of progress. Education made them ashamed of their dung and fish-gut trades – it was a far superior thing to sit at an office desk with a pen and ledger or to serve behind the counter of a Hamnavoe shop. The man who couldn't speak proper English was an inferior creature. Religion was Smilesian – heaven looked with favour on those who strove to improve themselves – unto him that hath shall be given. The novels that dribbled into the valley showed them Sir Sylvester and Lady Jasmine tangled in emotional delicacies very different (and, they tacitly assumed, superior) to their own primitive lustings and delights. The penny newspapers opened to them horizons wide as the world; they began, with a sense of fatuous freedom, to argue in the crofts about Gladstone's Irish policy and free trade versus protection; and the advertisements told them there was no illness, from toothache to consumption, that couldn't be cured with Holbrook's pills; and there was no dark place anywhere that couldn't be mapped and civilised and evangelised . . . A gramophone with a horn came to the valley, and the fiddle hung at the wall like a dry chrysalis. 'The Poor-boy-who-had-Got-On' became the new folk hero; Kirkwall Grammar School at that period was full of embryonic professors; the Orcadians have always been a people of high intelligence.

More and more the young people began to leave the valley.

Here and there a croft fell vacant, and after a fireless winter the roof fell in.

The notion of progress is a cancer that makes an elemental

community look better, and induces a false euphoria, while it drains the life out of it remorselessly.

The population thinned out and aged. One after another the houses were deserted. In the summer of 1952 there were only two boys, brothers, left in the valley among their elders. One morning, playing on a raft in the deepest part of the burn – while the oatfields ripened around them – they were both drowned. It seemed like the old Fate uttering final sentence over Rackwick.

Today there is only one farm left. The valley is littered with ruins. A few houses have been restored and Kirkwall and Stromness families live there at weekends. City people, sick of traffic and telephones, spend a whole summer in Rackwick. The lovely setting remains; artists, poets, composers take inspiration from pure uncluttered sources. It is a microcosm of gracious living, not yet entirely extinct.

I do not think Rackwick will remain empty for ever. It could happen that the atom-and-planet horror at the heart of our civilisation will scatter people again to the quiet beautiful fertile places of the world.

At Burnmouth the door hangs from a broken hinge
And the fire is out.

The windows of Shore empty sockets
And the hearth coldness.

At Bunnertoon the small drains are choked.
Thrushes nest in the chimney.

Stars shine through the roof beams of Scar.
No flame is needed
To warm ghosts and nettles and rats.

Greenhill is sunk in a new bog.
No kneeling woman
Blows red wind through squares of ancient bog.

The Moss is a tumble of stones.
That black stone
Is the stone where the hearth fire was rooted.

And at Midhouse among those flowers of flame
Bread and fish were baked.
That enchanted stone turned the blue lobster red.

In Crowsnest the sunken hearth
Was an altar for priests of legend,
Old seamen from the clippers with silken beards.

The three-toed pot at the wall of Park
Is lost to woman's cunning.
A slow fire of rust eats the cold iron.

The sheep drift through Reumin all winter.
Sheep and snow
Blanch fleetingly the black stone.

It is still there,
The flat stone in Winbrake where the water-pot stood,
But always the eye seeks the charred stone.

From that sacred stone the children of the valley
Drifted lovewards
And out of labour to the lettered kirkyard stone.

The fire beat like a heart in each house
From the first corner-stone
Till they led through the sagging lintel the last old one.

The poor and the good fires are all quenched.
Now, cold angel, keep the valley
From the bedlam and cinders of a Black Pentecost.

3

VIKINGS: 'THE TRANSFIXED DRAGON'

WARRIOR

MARTYR

CRUSADER

WARRIOR

THE THREE ships of Sigurd, Earl of Orkney, were lying at anchor in Kirk Hope in the south of Hoy when a small weather-scarred fleet entered the bay from the Pentland Firth. The captain was a Norwegian called Olaf Tryggvison who was now returning home after a very strange experience. During his cruise he had been baptised into Christianity in the Isles of Scilly – his soul changed overnight from a fate-blown wisp to a pearl of incalculable price. He sailed homeward, eager to enrich all the north with his revelation. The first big fish to swim into his net was Earl Sigurd in Kirk Hope, Hoy.

Their exchange of courtesies was brief. 'You will either become a Christian now', said Olaf Tryggvison, 'you and all your men, or I will comb your islands with sword and fire'.

'I will leave the decision in your hands', said Earl Sigurd. It was a canny answer; it meant that he had not been allowed to decide freely, and so his baptism was not entirely valid; but it was enough for Olaf Tryggvison. Earl Sigurd and the sailors had the waters of baptism poured on their bent heads. To make sure that there would be no back-sliding, Olaf

Tryggvison took Sigurd's young son Hund to Norway with him as a hostage.

So, just before the year A.D. 1000, Orkney became officially Christian.

It did not last. After a year or two the boy hostage Hund died in Norway. Besides that, Earl Sigurd was not attracted to Christianity. The old northern gods ruled from the abodes of ice and tempest. They uttered dark inscrutable decrees. To men in their few flickering years the wisdom of Odin and Thor appeared as fate, a difficult mystery, for we would have acted differently in this eventuality or that if our choice had been free; and yet – even earthly wisdom knew this – any free choice issuing out of an ignorance almost boundless – which earthly wisdom is, at best – would result in actions so weird and ludicrous that it was best not to contemplate such a 'tale told by an idiot'. Of only a few abstract qualities could a man be sure – of courage, for example, and of loyalty, and of generosity. These were the jewels that a man could save out of the flux. If you were lucky, perhaps some sagaman would set your actions in the horn and silver of his prose; that was the only kind of immortality a man could hope for. Since death was certain, it was best to meet it with a jest; the wry witty death-utterance is a commonplace in the sagas; and death in a battle or a siege, while a man was still young and strong, was certainly to be preferred to 'a straw death' – an old grey head wheezing and choking some winter with pneumonia, for example, in a shut-bed in Barra or Westray.

This was the ambience within which Earl Sigurd moved and acted. The new religion out of the east seemed to men like him incredible.

A birth in a stable, a wandering preaching life among hills and deserts, a death attended with every variety of humiliation and pain – Earl Sigurd did not see how a god would ever manifest himself in such a way. (It was only when the north Europeans saw Christ as the young hero conquering the dragon of death, as in *The Dream of the Rood*, that they began to take to the new religion. The great wars did not after all rage for ever in the world outside – a man's soul had its battlefields, its silent betrayals, its mute heroisms and victories.)

But Christ's charity meant nothing as yet to Earl Sigurd. You felt affection for the men who sailed with you and fought with you in English sea-ports and the straths of Scotland. You felt a sense of duty to your parents, which might or might not be touched with affection. You had a tenderness for your bed-mate. There was the child Hund, the hostage that the Christian Olaf Tryggvison had taken eastwards to Norway with him, and was now dead – Earl Sigurd felt a stir of pity and tenderness for that small ghost. But he did not and could not include in his charity strangers he had never seen, such as Frenchmen or Irishmen. After the death of Hund, Sigurd returned to the security of his ancient faith.

The decrees of fate were final, but it was possible for men to reach some kind of accommodation with fate; to influence to some extent its decisions, so that the outcome of any undertaking might be favourable rather than otherwise. The gods were not entirely deaf to mortal pleas and aspirations, but it was not just a simple matter of telling them, in the silence between heart-beats, what you wanted. Into the riddling region where gods and men negotiated only an elite could trespass – men who had made a long study of the black arts, professional enchanters and spell-binders, they were permitted to look into the seeds of fate and to see which would wither and which would flourish. Earl Sigurd's mother Edna was a priestess of these mysteries. For her son she had made a banner that, borne in battle, would bring him victory. Woven into the flag was a raven, symbol of Odin – the bird of memory and foresight, that knew what had happened and what is to happen. The banner had one drawback; whoever carried it would himself be cut down in battle. This was the

kind of reservation the gods revelled in. 'Yes,' they seemed
to say, 'you can have this boon and that, we permit it, it is
written down already in the book of fate, but on the other
hand, to show after all that a bond exists between gods and
men, you will have to grant us something in exchange. A
victorious standard, yes, very good, we freely grant it, but
the standard will be carried always by a dead man . . .' The
gods' answers to the beseechings of men were full of such
reservations and equivocations; so that, though your petition
might indeed be granted, it was often granted in such a way
that the invocation had perhaps better never been uttered in
the first place.

It was Sigurd's mother, the banner-weaver, who made the
superb reply to her son when he doubted that a battle against
Findlaec, Earl of Moray, might be too dangerous to under-
take, the odds against him being seven to one – 'I would have
brought you up in my wool-basket if I had known you
expected to live for ever'.

At Yule in the year 1013 Earl Sigurd entertained an important visitor at his hall in Orphir – Sigtrygg, king of Dublin.
Sigtrygg, who was a pagan, had for overlord Brian Boru,
High King of Ireland, a Christian; but he chafed even more
under the nagging of his mother, a ferocious woman who had
once been King Brian's wife and now nursed a devouring
hatred of him. (There have never been women in history like
the Norse women of the sagas; they seem more like savage
seabirds than women; once the cold glaucous eye fell on son
or lover or husband, these heroes ran meekly to obey their
smallest whim. These women stirred the cauldrons of hatred
generation by generation, when men would have let the fires
die. They threw one faint shadow at least into the Scandinavian nineteenth century: Hedda Gabler.)

Sigtrygg intended, he told Earl Sigurd, to raise an army

against King Brian, and he urgently invited the Orkney Earl to take part in the war. He regarded an alliance with Earl Sigurd as of such importance that he accepted Sigurd's terms at once – Brian's kingdom, and marriage with Sigtrygg's mother Kormlada, Besides, Sigurd was to be in the centre of the battle-array, as virtual commander-in-chief.

The Irish crown was too impossible to be true; even while he put his hand into Sigtrygg's hand the Earl knew that that offer, and probably the offer of the mother too, was little more than a symbol; Sigtrygg had not come all this way for a change of overlord or step-father. But the high honour of the battle-centre was quite another thing; once offered, it could not be withdrawn, it was a genuine tribute to Sigurd's battle-wit and bravery, and to the rare magic of his mother's weaving.

Besides, this war would be a supreme opportunity for Sigurd to avenge himself on the Christians for little Hund who had been taken from him into the shades.

The alliance was struck among the ale cups and the gnawed bones. Earl Sigurd and his army would be in Dublin for the rendezvous on Palm Sunday, 1014.

King Sigtrygg returned to Ireland to marshal forces for a spring war. Spurred on by his terrible mother, he tried to gain the support of two Viking chiefs, the brothers Brodir and Ospak, whose thirty ships were wintering near the Isle of Man.

Brodir, like Sigurd of Orkney, was a lapsed Christian – more, he had once been a deacon in holy orders. Sigtrygg, with apparent duplicity, offered Brodir the same rewards that he had offered to Sigurd – his mother in marriage and the kingship of Ireland. It was not duplicity; it was a cunning deployment of symbols; and recognised by all concerned as such.

This intricate subtle bargaining is a prelude to every war. All statesmen and commanders expect to participate in the ritual – a symbolical foretasting of the fruits of victory. One does not go cold into battle; one goes primed with prospects and promises and slogans, already agreed upon over a table in the lamplight. The precious symbols shine untarnished among the blood and slime. The great heroes dare not let their symbols go; if they do, for a single moment, their victories dwindle to an acre here and there honeycombed with corpses. Napoleon, reeling between the fires of Moscow and the Beresina ice, still clung to his imagined trophies – columns and laurels and law-books in a united Europe more glorious than Greece or Rome . . . So the Irish-Norse commanders arrange beforehand their symbolical chessmen – a sceptre, a princess, a harpsong – while the first trumpet call (and well they know it) will release horrors and degradations over which they have small control, and that will suck all their immaculate counters into the vortex . . . Sigtrygg's mother, and the high kingship of Ireland, were two prestigious symbols, no more. What in truth did Sigurd, or Brodir, want with an ageing harridan like Kormlada? Sigtrygg could not have expected to get away with lies like these; it was too dangerous, if the Earl of Orkney or the Viking ex-deacon had taken him seriously; for the whole underhanded transaction would come to light in the camaraderie before battle, and Sigtrygg's grand plan fall apart like an ill-stitched coat. Besides, how could a gadabout Viking, or the chief of a few northern islands, ever hope to become High King of Ireland? – neither the one nor the other could compel the allegiance of the Norse-Irish princes. Both Sigurd and Brodir knew – and Sigtrygg knew that they knew – that Sigtrygg and no other was to be lord of all Ireland after the victory. What made the Earl of Orkney fight then? Not the western world, or a woman; these were shadows. But courage, loyalty, generosity – these were to be plucked from the imminent bloody vortex . . . Sigurd wanted nothing but the centre of the battle and a place in the story. Brodir would settle for cart-loads of loot. Meantime all three accepted the symbols of their alliance – a throne and a woman – and two of them knew that they were being offered shadows. Earl Sigurd knew it; but in the Book of Fate the runes of what was to happen were written already. What if Sigtrygg and Brodir, and all the princes of Ireland, fell in the battle? Sigurd in the Minch, sailing south with his Orkneymen and his Icelanders, felt for a moment the touch of gold-and-emerald on his brow; then knew it was a shadow; dismissed it, and looked forward only to the valour and the loyalty and the generosity . . .

The other Viking leader, Ospak (Brodir's brother) was a pagan, but he had been impressed by the stories that had lately come out of Ireland regarding the character of King Brian Boru – a man, it seemed, of a sweet and holy and gentle life, who had won the love of all his people except for a few such upstarts as Sigtrygg of Dublin and the King of Leinster. Ospak said flatly, 'I will not fight against so good a king as Brian.'

Brodir and Ospak split up their forces at once. Ospak went to offer his services to King Brian.

Both armies assembled for battle between Howth and the Liffey on Palm Sunday. The manoeuvering for position, the ordering of the armies with due regard to precedence, went on all week. On the morning of Good Friday, all was ready; the great looms began to hum.

Clontarf is one of the key European battles, as vital to the course of history as Lepanto or Waterloo or Stalingrad, and yet we know hardly anything about it. We know that, according to the Yule promise given to him, Sigurd was in the centre of the 'pagan' array with his Orkneymen and a company of young exciled Icelanders who had been at the burning of Njal the winter before. On one side of Earl Sigurd – but so vague are the dispositions that we don't know whether to his left or to his right – were Brodir and his

Vikings, and Sigtrygg the rebel king at his other flank. Opposite Earl Sigurd, in the centre of the 'Christian' army, was Kerthialfad, King Brian's loved foster-son. Brodir's Vikings were opposed by Brian's brother Ulf Hreda (literally, Wolf the Quarrelsome) and Ospak and the sons of Brian faced Sigtrygg of Dublin.

King Brian himself, seeing that it was Good Friday, refused to fight, in imitation of Christ who had suffered all things uncomplaining on that day. He stood all through the onset weaponless behind a wall of shields.

We can guess only crudely at the actual course of the battle. It seems – reading the saga accounts that are usually so factual and reliable – as if the men taking part in it were only puppets, and that the real battle was fought out by supernatural beings, the heavenly legions against the principalities and powers of darkness. Signs and portents showered from heaven on the warriors; the whole action is ringed round with supernatural masques and tableaux, such as the assault on Brodir on three sequent nights before Clontarf by showers of boiling blood, swords and axes fighting of their own accord, iron-taloned ravens. There was the Earl of Orkney's raven banner. There was Brodir's enchanted armour that no sword or arrow could bite on. There was the web of entrails woven by the Valkyries. There was the Clontarf blood on the priest's stole in Iceland, a thousand miles away, when Mass was being celebrated.

The battle was between Christ and Odin for the soul of Ireland.

Yet there was no clear distinction of faith between the opposing commanders. Brodir and Sigurd were technically Christians; as a man in minor holy orders Brodir must have assisted at Mass in churches all over the west. Ospak, who fought on the Christian side, was a pagan. Brian's brother Ulf, if we are to judge by the little private ritual he carried out after the victory, was a sadistic beast even by eleventh-century Viking standards. Only King Brian at the shield-wall seems an 'alter Christus', a sacrificial victim, the dove in the storm's centre.

The battle began with Brodir and his Vikings moving against Ulf. The attack broke against the Irish shields. Brodir and his shattered column retreated into a wood bordering the battle-field. From that green sanctuary Brodir watched the clashing of the great looms and the crimson growing web.

On the other side of the field Ospak led the assault on Sigtrygg, and broke through after a hard struggle. Ospak's two sons were killed and Ospak himself was badly wounded.

The main action was fought in the centre, between the forces of Sigurd of Orkney and Kerthialfad. The sagaman's account of the end of the battle is a blend of humour and horror and compassion.

Earl Sigurd had a hard battle against Kerthialfad. Kerthialfad advanced with such a rush that he scattered all the men in the front rank, and smashed Earl Sigurd's army as far as the banner, and killed the man who carried it.

Earl Sigurd got another man to carry the standard, and the hard battle went on.

Kerthialfad immediately struck down this man and killed him and also the men round about him, one after the other.

Then Earl Sigurd ordered Thorstein the son of Hall of the Side (an Icelander) to bear the banner. Thorstein was just about to lift it when Asmund the White said, 'Don't carry the banner! Everyone who carries it gets killed.'

'Hrafn the Red!' cried Earl Sigurd, 'you carry the banner.'

'Carry your own devil,' said Hrafn.

The Earl said then, 'Certainly the beggar should carry his own bag,' and he tore banner from pole and stuffed it under his cloak.

Soon afterwards, Asmund the White was killed, and then a spear transfixed the Earl. . . .

Then the whole army broke.

Thorstein, son of Hall of the Side, stood still when everybody else fled, and tied his shoe-string.

Kerthialfad asked him why he hadn't run with the others.

'Because,' said Thorstein, 'I can't get home tonight. I live out in Iceland.'

Kerthialfad spared him.

Hrafn the Red was pursued into a river. He looked down and thought he saw the torments of hell and devils waiting to drag him there.

Hrafn said, 'Your dog, Saint Peter, has run to Rome twice. He would run a third time if you let him.'

Then the devils released him and Hrafn got across the river.

Brodir saw that King Brian's army was in full pursuit, and only a few men were left round the shield wall.

He rushed out of the wood, broke through the shield wall, and struck at the king.

The boy Takt threw his arm in the way, and the stroke took it off and the king's head, but the king's blood fell on the lad's stump and at once the stump healed up.

Then Brodir shouted, 'Everybody should know that Brodir killed Brian!'

Men ran after the pursurers and told them King Brian had fallen. Ulf Hreda and Kerthialfad turned back at once.

They surrounded Brodir and his men, and threw branches on them; in this way Brodir was taken alive.

Ulf Hreda cut open his belly, and led him round and round a tree-trunk, and so unwound all his entrails, and he did not die before he was completely gutted.

Brodir's men were all killed.

*

It was one of the bloodiest battles in history. According to one Irish chronicle, the soldiers were cut down like corn in a harvest field.

In Caithness that day a man called Darraud saw twelve horsewomen riding into a hillside. He followed where they seemed to go, and saw through a rock-cleft twelve women setting up a loom, and singing.

> The warp is stretched
> For warrior's death.
> The weft in the loom
> Drips with blood.
> The battle darkens.
> Under our fingers
> The tapestry grows,
> Red as heart's blood
> Blue as corpses,
> The web of battle.
>
> What is this woof?
> The guts of men.
> The weights on the warp
> Their slaughtered heads.
> These are our spindles,
> Blood-splashed spears.
> An iron loom-frame;
> And the reels, arrows;
> With swords for shuttles
> This war-web we weave,
> Valkyries weaving
> The web of victory . . .

The song shuttles on for eleven verses, a lengthening tissue of ghastliness.

The imagination of the Scandinavian peoples was branded for centuries with the horror of Clontarf. Seven and a half centuries after the battle the minister of North Ronaldsay in Orkney read aloud to some of his people Thomas Gray's paraphrase of the Valkyries' song. The islanders heard the first few stanzas out, then told their minister that they knew the poem already in their old Norn tongue.

Now the storm begins to lower,
(Haste, the loom of Hell prepare.)
Iron-sleet of arrowy shower
Hurtles in the darken'd air.

Glitt'ring lances are the loom,
Where the dusky harp we strain,
Weaving many a Soldier's doom,
Orkney's woe, and *Randver*'s bane.

See the griesly texture grow,
('Tis of human entrails made,)
And the weights, that play below,
Each a gasping Warrior's head.

Shafts for shuttles, dipt in gore,
Shoot the trembling cords along.
Sword, that once a Monarch bore,
Keep the tissue close and strong.

Mista black, terrific Maid,
Sangrida, and *Hilda* see,
Join the wayward work to aid:
'Tis the woof of victory.

Ere the ruddy sun be set
Pikes must shiver, javelins sing,
Blade with clattering buckler meet,
Hauberk crash, and helmet ring.

(Weave the crimson web of war)
Let us go, and let us fly,

Where our Friends the conflict share,
Where they triumph, where they die.

As the paths of fate we tread,
Wading thro' th'ensanguin'd field:
Gondula, and *Geira*, spread
O'er the youthful King your shield.

We the reins to slaughter give,
Ours to kill, and ours to spare:
Spite of danger he shall live.
(Weave the crimson web of war) . . .

Low the dauntless Earl is laid,
Gor'd with many a gaping wound;
Fate demands a nobler head;
Soon a King shall bite the ground.

Long his loss shall Eirin weep,
Ne'er again his likeness see;
Long her strains in sorrow steep,
Strains of Immortality!

Horror cover all the heath,
Clouds of carnage blot the sun.
Sisters, weave the web of death;
Sisters, cease, the work is done . . .

Sisters, hence with spurs of speed;
Each her thundering faulchion wield,
Each bestride her sable steed.
Hurry, hurry to the field.

Never were the great war heroes so savagely mocked; and
the mockery echoes back and fore through history. What
(the song asks) are Alexander, Caesar, Charles the Twelfth,
Napoleon, but servants of the Valkyries, driving caravans
loaded with vats of blood and gut-webs through the nations

and the centuries? – not a threshold in Europe but holds a bloody bargaining, generation by generation, with these traffickers. Sigurd, Earl of Orkney, was a small-time huckster in comparison. He wrapped his mother's flag round his body and compared himself to a ragman and with that flash of insight was out of the story.

Into the Valkyries' loom passed the blood and guts of all the men who had fallen at Clontarf, for the ghastly wardrobes of history to be restocked and refurbished. Brodir, the renegade deacon, had not needed to wait for death to be a part of the web; his entrails decorated the tree while he was still alive, in a hideous parody of Judas Iscariot whose bowels gushed out under greenery and birdsong.

We must think of King Brian Boru's head and heart as being exempt from the Valkyries' hands. History has other looms, where a Seamless Garment is being worked on. The shuttles fly perpetually, secretly, silently, in little islands where the brothers plough and fish and pray; in lonely oratories; in great churches from Galway to Byzantium.

In the next pages we shall see the working of another section of the Seamless Garment in even more remarkable circumstances. It happened in Orkney, about a century later.

MARTYR

EARL SIGURD who was swallowed up at Clontarf had two great-grandsons, cousins – Hakon Paulson and Magnus Erlendson – and in due time, after the death of their fathers, they inherited jointly the Earldom of Orkney.

How is it possible for two rulers to wear a single coat-of-state?

This double, sometimes multiple rule, was the curse of Norse overlordship in the islands. There was no primogeniture, all a man's sons inherited power and property equally; and the result, in the high places of Orkney, was a continuing chaos. Yet nobody thought of challenging this system. The kings of Norway actively encouraged it. Nominally, the king in the east was overlord of Orkney, but in actuality Orkney was prosperous enough and distant enough to be half independent. A single strong earl of Orkney, like Thorfinn (Sigurd's son), could give a half-cynical acquiesence to the king's overlordship, while he pursued his own private aggrandisement in Scotland and Ireland and the Hebrides. But once a strong earl died and two or more sons inherited the earldom jointly, the inevitable happened. After a year or

69

two they quarrelled about lands or revenues or responsibilities; the stronger one took over all the islands; the rejected one sailed eastwards to Norway and laid his cause before the king. The king was always sympathetic, supplied him with ships and men and money. Next spring a war fleet descended like hawks from the east, and the islands were aflame from end to end. Whatever the outcome, the king of Norway invariably established himself once more as lord of Orkney too. The earl became his man and ate his salt.

Sigurd himself had had four sons; there was violent conflict, blood and exhaustion over the whole community, before the youngest of them, Thorfinn, emerged as sole earl. This Thorfinn was the most powerful ruler that Orkney ever had, 'a tall black ugly hawk-nosed sharp-featured man'. By good luck he lived to be over seventy, a great age in those days, and he extended the earldom deep into the Highlands and Western Isles of Scotland. In the latter part of his life he made a pilgrimage to Rome, travelling on horseback over the Alps, in company – it is said – with King Macbeth of Scotland. Macbeth was so relieved at getting absolution from the Pope that 'he scattered money like seed to the poor of Rome . . .'

Earl Thorfinn built his palace on a steep green tidal holm called The Brough on the north-west of Birsay. The sea rises and falls about the island, twice a day, Next to the palace was Orkney's first cathedral church, with a new bishop, William, 'a clerk of Paris,' in residence. Some walls of those gracious buildings are still standing.

Earl Thorfinn left two sons, Paul and Erlend, joint earls. They get a few sentences in the saga, then they die in Norway, wards of the king there, and are gathered into history, gentle ghosts.

The son of Paul was called Hakon, the surviving son of Erlend was called Magnus.

About the early days of Hakon Paulson there is nothing remarkable; he fitted easily into his time. He was an energetic able young man. He would have learned the skills of the nobility: falconry, hunting, navigation, verse-making, chess, sword-play, horsemanship. His ambition, like all young noblemen was to leave a great name behind him, to shine in some saga as brave and wise and generous. He was a Christian; he was baptised in the font at The Brough; he went to Mass on Sundays and holy days and knelt devoutly before Christ the Hero. But fame in history was probably the only kind of immortality this young Norseman believed in: a resurrection in the word.

The other child who issued from the same font about the same time, Magnus Erlendson, learned no doubt the same arts of chivalry as his cousin Hakon Paulson, and was – we may believe – equally accomplished. He carried his hawk on his wrist to the hill, he could turn an impromptu lyric, he was useful in a duel. We cannot get a clear picture of the man because his monkish biographer has smudged the outline with conventional pious platitudes.

Saint Magnus, the island Earl, was a most outstanding man, tall, virile, with a vivacious expression, virtuous in his doings, lucky in war, wise, witty, quick with his tongue, noble-minded, generous, magnanimous, a sagacious councillor, extremely popular. He was pleasant and courteous in his talk to good and well disposed men, but hard and pitiless to bandits and Vikings. He had those men put to death – harriers of freemen and the common people. He had murderers and thieves imprisoned, and sentenced rich as well as poor for robbery, theft, all kinds of lawlessness. He let no bias influence his judgements; divine justice was more important to him than earthly rank. He was generous to chiefs and influential people, but always he dealt the greatest measure of generosity to the poor. In all things he obeyed strictly God's commandments, and he mortified his flesh in many ways which in his shining life were known to God but hidden from men. He made clear his faith in this way: he paid court to a high-born Scottish girl and married her; he lived with her for ten years, and satisfied neither his own lust nor hers, and was pure and unsullied from fleshly taint. If he felt tempted he bathed in cold water and prayed for God's help. There were many other good traits and princely virtues that he showed to God but kept hid from men . . .

In fact, the bones of Magnus in Kirkwall Cathedral show him to have been a rather small man, not tall as the scribe insists. The complete portrait therefore falls apart, like a loose thread unravelling a badly-knitted garment; such as cold water as a preservative of chastity. Medieval hagiographers revelled in extravagant manifestations. What it meant was this, perhaps: when Magnus lusted, like other men, and the lust proved a distraction, he would go into a church and dip his fingers in holy water and cross himself. This simple action has been known to quieten, at one time or another, all of the seven deadly sins. On the other hand, like many generous people, he may have been so excessively tormented that he imposed harsh restraints on himself.

But out of the pietistic fog a strange disconcerting figure emerges. The events that gather about him are so extraordinary, and were witnessed by so many people, and were enacted in such a hard light, that there is no faking of the record.

There is one episode in his youth that ought to have forewarned those in the high places of Norway and Orkney that a man was growing up among them who would not fit easily into the accepted patterns.

While the brothers Paul and Erlend ruled Orkney, King Magnus of Norway came from the east with a powerful force . . . He took Earl Paul and Earl Erlend and sent them east to Norway . . . King Magnus then proceeded to the

Hebrides. Magnus and Erling, sons of Earl Erlend, and Hakon son of Earl Paul, went with him.

When King Magnus came to the Hebrides he began to raid, in Lewis at the start, and he conquered it. He conquered all the Hebrides in the course of that cruise . . . From there he sailed south to the Welsh coast. He fought a great battle in Menai Strait against two Welsh Earls, Hugh the Stout (Earl of Shrewesbury) and Hugh the Proud (Earl of Chester).

While the men were unsheathing their weapons in readiness for the battle, Magnus Erlendson sat down in the well aft and did nothing in the way of arming himself. The king asked him why he was sitting down. He said he had no quarrel with any man there, 'and so I won't fight'. The king said, 'Go down below, don't lie here among men's feet, if you're afraid to fight. I don't think this comes out of religious conviction'.

Magnus took a psalter and sang through all the fighting, but he did not take shelter. It was a long stern battle, hurling of missiles and sword-clash. For long it was uncertain how the scales would tilt. King Magnus was armed with a bow. He had an archer from Helgeland at his side. Hugh the Proud fought bravely. He was plated with mail so that only his eyes were showing. King Magnus ordered the Helgeland man to shoot at Hugh at the same time as he himself shot. One arrow struck the nose-plate, the other went into the skull through his eye – that was said to be the king's bolt. Hugh the Proud fell on the spot.

Then the Welsh fled, having lost a multitude of men. For King Magnus it was a great victory, although many good men had fallen and more were wounded . . .

King Magnus took over Angelsea, the most southerly territory conquered by any king of Norway up to then: a third part of Wales.

King Magnus then returned along the south coast of Scotland.

King Magnus had previously appointed Magnus Erlend-son to be his trencher-bearer; his duty to wait always at the king's table. But after the Menai battle King Magnus took a violent dislike to him and said he was a coward. Magnus had come through the battle shelterless but unwounded . . .

'I have no quarrel with any man here' – it was the first time in the recorded history of the north that that remark had been made. It has been made, sporadically, ever since, nowadays with increasing urgency. Some day soon all men everywhere will have to speak it, if the nations are not to be involved in a final holocaust; and after that, perhaps, the saints will inherit the earth.

Long before, a shepherd boy had struck consolation from his harp for an embattled king: the peace of Jerusalem. The King of Norway could not hear it for Valkyrie music.

What kind of a community lived in Orkney at the be-ginning of the twelfth century?

The eastern horizon belonged to the King of Norway. No other sail broke that circle.

There was a group of chiefs and large farmers who adminis-tered their considerable estates, and lived in the large Bu farms and long-halls in fertile tracts along the island coasts or beside the lochs; men of some culture, who relished a skaldic verse – those dense intricate weavings of kenning and allitera-tion – and the swift clean line of a saga. They might have one or two ships that traded into Norway or Scotland, or, as Vikings, plundered the south twice a year, after the spring sowing and the harvest.

Arni, Thorvald, Sven, Paul, Grettir, Harald,
The *Sea Wolf* is out of the shed, new tar on her hull.

The rollers are under the keel.
The women have put ale, salt meat, and bread on board.
As soon as the wave runs clean from Birsay
We will leave the Orkneys behind us,
The scarred hills and the creeled sounds,
And tonight we will anchor at the mouth of a Scottish river.
Our voyage lies east this year.
We have heard of such towns – Aberdeen, Grimsby,
    London,
And the merchants who live in tall houses.
The churches have had enough of our swords,
And the girls who weave their words into curse or spell.
Our voyage does not lie west this spring
Among holiness and drifts of rain.
There are few chalices left in those islands.
It is time merchants knew about us.
We will be back in time for the corn harvest.
You women, see that the scythes are sharp and the barns
    swept,
And the ale thick with honey.
We are tired of broken coast-lines.
This summer we deal in wool and useful currency.
They are not too beautiful, the girls in the east.

There were the peasants in every island, a host of them –
Mans and Sigurth and Amund – of mixed Norse and Pictish
blood, who year after year dug and drained and reclaimed a
new bit of tilth and pasture from the grouse-haunted hills.
They, too, suffered a sea change in summer, and were
generally at the sacking of some Irish church or English
seaport, and came home with wounds and bits of silver on
them.

There were the fishermen – Leif Saltfinger, Gunnar Creel –
who might get one fish out of seven to themselves, after all
their debts and dues were paid.

The island women must be mentioned too – Hild and Gerd and Biorg – who lived between the well and the fire. Busy with spinning, grinding, churning, they turned perpetual wheels of wood and stone and milk. They obeyed implicitly the rhythms of fruition in the fields and in their own bodies, the great wheels of moon and sun.

There were small communities of monks – Colm and Benedict and Simon – who wore the long bright coats and lived frugally in islands like Eynhallow or Papay, and sang season by season their Masses and litanies and office.

There were the mendicants – Jock and Mary – the frayed fringe of every society, lower even than the thralls; the houseless heads and unfed sides that Lear pitied in his madness. These outcasts were increasing yearly, as the islands grew poorer.

In a wholesome society the different estates are stitched together in a single garment: the warmth and comfort and well-being of the people, a symbol too of their identity and their ethos. Their language, their work, their customs, all they think and do and say, decide the style and cut of the coat. The simplest bit of social intercourse – a conversation at a cross-roads, the selling of a pig, a kiss in the darkness – puts in another stitch, does its bit in holding the tribe together and ensuring its survival. It is at best a frayed improvised thing, always coming unstuck, that never adequately covers the whole commonwealth; there is a perpetual tugging and bickering between this estate and that for a greater share of the coat – the landlords saying they must increase the rent; the fishermen left some winters with only a cod's head from the division of the seven fish; the women in a thin year worn with the turning of fruitless wheels – but the slow ponderous womb-wheel never failed to cast a new hunger into the cradle, year by year.

The garment that was necessary for the welfare of the community was never broad enough or thick enough; and northern winters are cold; and with the incessant civil wars between rival earls, generation by generation, the garment was now hardly better than tatters upon crossed sticks in a January furrow.

There was another coat, very precious and inviolable; their fathers and their grandfathers before them had imagined it and had given it to the looms of history; and this heavy heraldic ceremonial coat was not finished, nor could they imagine a final shape to it, because their sons would still be at the weaving of it. Being woven, it could not be sundered. This was the coat-of-state that the earl wore when he gave his decision in the assembly and put his seal on a new decree. The mystical hierarchic unfinished coat-of-state had now to be worn, somehow, by two new earls, Hakon Paulson and Magnus Erlendson.

There was a third coat; as yet only the monks in lonely islands wore it – the long white weave of innocence that they must have ready for the bridal-feast of Christ. *Consider the lilies of the field, how they grow* – sang Colm and Benedict and Simon – *they labour not, neither do they spin, but I say to you, that not even Solomon in all his glory was arrayed as one of these. Now if God so clothe the grass of the field, which is today, and tomorrow is cast into the oven, how much more you, O ye of little faith.* . . .

But it was the first garment, the coat of diurnal hand-to-mouth existence, that in the opening years of the twelfth century concerned everybody in Orkney, rich and poor; for it had been torn and bloodied with centuries of civil strife, shredded thin with taxation, and the danger was that soon they would return to their pristine savagery, 'poor bare forked animals'. The quality of life had become exceedingly patched and poor. The earls had neglected their people for too long; they had given most of their wealth and energy to war, to the Valkyries' tissue of guts-and-blood; and it was deep winter at all seasons of the year.

77

It was stark winter – time for history to become poetry, drama, a fertility dance.

The cousins Magnus and Hakon ruled and guarded the land for a while, so long as they were friends. A poem tells how they fought against the chief called Donald, son of Earl Duncan, their own second cousin, and defeated him.

They killed a chief called Thorbjorn in Burra Firth, Shetland; burning his house over his head. The poem describes many other affairs that they both had a hand in; here they are only touched on.

When the cousins had ruled the land for a time, a group of mischief-makers – this often happens, and is a possibility always – contrived to come between them.

Two of Earl Hakon's men especially were named as the chief breakers of harmony, Sigurd and Sighvat Socks. Slander grew and flourished on the tongues of men like them to such an extent that the cousins gathered forces and opposed one another, Earl against Earl, with imposing armies. They converged on Hrossey (the main island) and met at the place of the Thing (assembly). Once arrived there, they drew up forces for battle.

Nearly all the chief men were with the earls, including a number of mutual friends; these did their best to make peace. Many, brave and well-intentioned, mediated between them. This confrontation was during Lent, not long before Palm Sunday. Because so many friends made it their business to keep peace, and refused to back up one so that the other would be put in the wrong, the earls agreed to a treaty, solemnly, their right hands clasped in friendship.

Time passed. Earl Hakon, manoeuvring for an advantage, proposed a meeting on a day to be fixed between himself and Earl Magnus to seal their friendship and ratify their recently-made treaty – nothing would break that. This meeting was to be in the island of Egilsay, in the Easter week of next spring.

This proposal pleased Earl Magnus . . . Each Earl was to have two ships and an equal number of men. Both vowed to keep the treaty-terms that the best councillors from both sides would hammer out meantime.

Easter passed. Each prepared for the meeting. Earl Magnus summoned all the men he thought most fair-minded and well-disposed to both cousins. He had two ships and the exactly stipulated number of men. He got ready for sea and steered towards Egilsay.

They rowed in calm placid water. A wave surged up under the ship the Earl was steering and broke in spindrift over the Earl's bench. His men were astonished at that – a wave breaking in a calm sea where no wave had been known to break before, and in deep water too!

The Earl said, 'No wonder you're surprised at this miracle or omen, whatever it is. It looks like a sign of my death. Perhaps the prophecy about Earl Hakon is beginning to unfold – it was said that Earl Paul's son would commit a very foul crime. Let's not deceive ourselves – my cousin Hakon has no intention of playing fair at this meeting. That's my opinion.'

A heart-heaviness fell on the Earl's men when he spoke of the short life before him. They urged him to save himself, and to trust Earl Hakon no further.

Earl Magnus answers, 'The voyage will continue. God's will be done . . .'

Now we turn to Earl Hakon, He called up a great force and had eight warships, completely manned for action. When the army gathered Earl Hakon told them what he meant to do. He would arrange things with Earl Magnus, at their meeting, in such a way that there would not be two earls in Orkney afterwards. A good number of his men were openly pleased; evil suggestions were added.

The loudest mouths belonged to that bad pair, Sigurd and Sighvat Socks.

The men plied their oars vigorously, cleaving the urgent water. Havard Gunnison was in the Earl's ship – he was Hakon's chief adviser; a relative and a good friend to both earls. Hakon had hidden the plot from him; he knew Havard would have no part in it. When Havard knew the Earl's mind, and that it was firmly made up, he leapt from his ship and swam to a deserted island . . .

Earl Magnus with his company arrived in Egilsay first. They saw Earl Hakon advancing with his eight ships. They knew then that the nets were spread. Earl Magnus walked inland with his men. He went into the church to pray, a night-long vigil. His men offered to guard him. The Earl answered, 'I won't put your lives in danger. Our peace is to do God's will.' His men felt then that his words, at the time of the bursting wave, were coming true. It was certainly not to save his life that he sought sanctuary. He prayed earnestly that his will be swallowed up in God's will. He asked for a Mass to be sung for him. He received holy communion.

Next morning, early, he left the church. There were two others with him. He went down to a secret place at the shore by another road. There again he contended with God.

Hakon and his men went ashore in the morning. They ran first to the church. They turned it inside out, but did not find the Earl. Then they began to comb the whole island for him. When Earl Magnus saw that, he shouted to them and let them know exactly where he was – they should look no further. Then Hakon spotted him; he and his men leapt down, yelling and clashing their weapons.

Earl Magnus was on his knees when they came where he was: he had not yet accepted the chalice. He crossed himself; then said resolutely to Earl Hakon, 'That was a bad thing, cousin, to go back on your promises. I hope fervently that your action comes from other men's evil and not your own. I will offer you three ways out of your faithlessness that do not involve the spilling of blood. Choose one way'.

Hakon's men asked what his offers were.

'This first,' said the Earl. 'I will travel south to Rome, or out to Palestine, and I will visit holy places. I will take two ships well equipped and manned. That pilgrimage will be for the benefit of both our souls. I will never return to the Orkneys while I live. This I swear.'

Hakon and his men immediately turned this down.

Earl Magnus then said, 'My life is in your hands. I have sinned exceedingly in the eye of God, and so I must do penance. But when or how I die is not for you to say. Send me, then, into Scotland. We have relatives there and mutual friends. Let me be held there under restriction and guard, with two warders to keep an eye on me always. Take what steps you think necessary to prevent any escape'.

They refused this at once, showing many reasons why it was impossible.

Magnus said, 'I offer you one last choice. I am thinking more of your souls, God knows, than my life. For you this is still better than murder – to cripple my body in any way you choose, or tear out my eyes, and then let me rot in some black prison.'

Earl Hakon said, 'I accept that solution, I ask for nothing more.'

The chiefs gathered round. They said to Earl Hakon, 'We intend to kill one or other of you now. From this day on you shall not rule this land together'.

Earl Hakon answered, 'If you're so set on this outcome, kill him – I would rather be a ruler and statesman than suddenly a corpse.'

Holdbodi, a reliable Hebridean chief, reported their actual dialogue; he was one of the two men with Earl Magnus when they took him.

81

Earl Magnus was as carefree as a man bidden to a feast, whose last feeling is hatred or anger. In the silence after the talking, he uttered another prayer; covering his face with his hands and shedding happy tears before God.

When Saint Magnus the Earl was condemned to death, Hakon ordered Ofeig his standard-bearer to be the executioner. Ofeig refused, very angrily. Then he ordered Lifolf his cook to kill Magnus. Lifolf began to sob loudly.

Earl Magnus said to him, 'You mustn't make a scene for a thing like this. You'll be a famous man for this day's work. Pull yourself together. You'll get my clothes – that's the old invariable custom. Don't be afraid either. You're not doing this because you want to do it. You're being forced to do it. There the blame lies.'

After saying that, the Earl took off his kirtle and gave it to Lifolf. He asked time for a last prayer; it was allowed him.

He prostrated himself on the ground. He offered himself for a sacrifice. He prayed for himself and his friends, then for his enemies and his murderers. He forgave utterly and completely those who were about to trespass into his very life. He confessed his sins; he prayed that he might be purged of them by the outpouring of his blood. Again he commended his soul into God's keeping. He beseeched the angels to meet his soul and bear it safe into the sanctuary of heaven. Then, a friend of God, he was led out to execution. He said to Lifolf, 'Stand in front of me. Swing the axe down hard, let the wound be on my forehead. I am an Earl, not a thief – my head mustn't be chopped off. Be brave, poor fellow. God will show you mercy – I have prayed for that too.'

He crossed himself. He offered his body to the axe. A single stroke took him flush on the forehead; and, a peregrine spirit, he shook this world from him.

The place up to that time had been a waste of moss and stone. But soon afterwards – so precious was Magnus to

God – green grass grew over the murder spot. This was God's way of showing that it was a holy death; that now Magnus was caught up into another intensity. This is one image of heaven: green pastures in the Land of the Ever-Young.

Earl Hakon refused permission for the Earl to be carried into the church.

Earl Magnus and Earl Hakon had been Earls of Orkney for seven years.

Thora, Magnus's mother, had asked them both to a feast. They were to go straight to her when they had sealed the treaty and returned from Egilsay. Earl Hakon came to the feast, after the killing of Magnus the Earl. Thora herself waited on the Earl and his men, and served them with drink. The Earl began to be drunk. Then she stood before him and said, 'You've come here alone, my lord. I expected two of you. Now you must gladden me in the eyes of God and men. Be my son (I have no other) and I will be your mother (you have none). I beg you then, out of charity, to have Magnus carried into the church. Treat my prayer the way you wish God to treat your soul on the Day of Judgement.'

The Earl fell silent and thought over what she had said. His sins troubled him in the midst of her gentle tears and entreaties for her son to have sanctuary. He looked at her, and wept, and said, 'Bury your son where you like.'

Then Earl Magnus was carried over to Birsay and buried in Christ's Kirk that Earl Thorfinn had built.

Next winter a holy light was often seen shining over his grave. People began to invoke him if they were in any danger and at once their prayers were answered. Also, a holy fragrance hung about his grave, and that cured many sick people. The sick of Orkney and Shetland began to make pilgrimages; they kept vigil at the grave of Saint Magnus the Earl and all their troubles were cured. But this could not be spoken of openly while Earl Hakon was alive.

At that time William was Bishop of Orkney – the first bishop the islands had. His cathedral was Christ's Kirk in Birsay. For seventy-six years William was bishop. For a long time he gave no credence to the sanctity of Earl Magnus.

After the killing, Earl Hakon became ruler of all Orkney. He forced all who had been Earl Magnus's men up to that time to become his sworn men. He became a great chief. He placed heavy penalties on the friends of Earl Magnus whom he considered to have played most part against him.

The saga-man is still obsessed with foreshadowings of fate, and the revising monk has been assiduous in putting haloes about the head of the hero. But the story remains solid and impressive; no one could have invented the psalter in the Welsh battle, or the tears of Lifolf the cook-executioner, or the conversation between Hakon and Magnus's mother.

The Battle of Clontarf and the Martyrdom of Saint Magnus are both set in the season of The Passion and Easter. The actors move about under the Cross. The fearful song of the Valkyries after the battle, about the garment of war woven from entrails, is not unlike the medieval hymns that picture Christ in his Passion, clothed in wounds and blood.

Clontarf was fought on Good Friday. It was Easter Monday when Magnus came to the stony field in Egilsay. To Hakon was made over entire now the heraldic coat-of-state. Magnus gave his clothes to Lifolf and knelt on the stone and went naked (it seemed) into the ecstasies of death. Yet all through history the shuttles are flying, perpetually, secretly, silently. The wedding garment, the shirt of invisible fire, is being woven – in little islands where the brothers plough and fish and pray; in lonely oratories; in great churches from Galway to Byzantium; and now, again, on a martyr-stone in a cold northern island.

Clontarf is all darkness and horror. What remained after the fall of the axe in Egilsay was a sense of boundless release, an entire people raised from the grave of its history, a corn-stalk bursting from a choked furrow.

'Earl Magnus was as carefree as a man bidden to a feast.' . . . The Bridegroom had no need to say to such a one, 'Friend, where is thy wedding garment?' . . . And the darkness outside was dappled with virgin-flames.

It was not possible, either, to fake the miracles that increased like ears of corn, like fish in the net, after the death of Magnus. The names of the sick people who were healed at the shrine of the saint, first in Birsay and afterwards in Kirkwall, were set out in order like a roll-call, together with their occupations and islands, and the cures effected: Bergfinn Skatison, landowner in Shetland, cured of blindness; Sigurd and Thorbjorn, two of Bergfinn's servants, cured of broken legs; Halfdan, Bergfinn's son, and Amundi Illugison, cured of leprosy; Sigurd from Fetlar, Shetland, cured of a deformed hand; Thorbjorn Gyrdson of Shetland, cured of lunacy; Thord Dragonskull, another of Bergfinn's servants, cured of 'raving madness'; Sigrid Sigurds – daughter of Sand, Shetland, cured of blindness; Sigurd Tandrison from Dale, Shetland, cured of 'devil-possession'. An Orkney woman called Groa was restored to her right mind; 'she stayed at the shrine the rest of her life, praising God.' In the course of a single night twenty-four sick men were cured.

The sceptical French-educated Bishop William was involved, against all his inclinations.

One summer Bishop William took ship to Norway. He delayed his return and made landfall in Shetland in late autumn. There was a gale-force contrary wind, but the Bishop wouldn't stay; he wanted to get home. The storm gathered and burst. It was full winter.

The helmsman mentioned a certain exchange to the

Bishop – a fair wind for the exhumation of Earl Magnus's relics.

The Bishop said Yes, if the storm allowed him to sing Mass in his cathedral the next Sunday.

The vow was made. The wind slackened and swung behind them. They sailed fast to Orkney. The Bishop sang his Mass at home on Sunday.

The Bishop seems, on reflection, to have thought a good wind was probably due in any case, for Magnus's bones lay undisturbed. In the web of being, spiritual and corporal are close-woven; Bishop William had to endure blindness and stumbling and God-cry before the relics were unearthed. With his new eyes the Bishop saw that 'the bones were clean and shining. A knuckle-bone was taken and tried three times in fire that had been blessed; it was not consumed, it glittered like gold, and some say it melted to the shape of a crucifix ... The body was enshrined over the altar. On St Lucy's Day that happened. Magnus had been twenty-one years buried . . .'

But the truest sign of the martyrdom appeared in the abundant horn of peace that tilted over the islands.

Some years after that, Hakon journeyed abroad. He went south to Rome; there the Pope absolved him from the sin of his deed. He voyaged on to Jerusalem. He visited the holy relics there and bathed in the River Jordan – the things pilgrims usually do.

Then he returned to his native land, lord of Orkney. He was a good ruler, and kept his earldom in peace. He made new laws in Orkney which the freemen considered to be a great improvement on former laws. They approved of him and his popularity grew. In the end the Orkneymen wanted only Hakon for their leader, and his son after him.

Alone, as he was meant to do, Hakon Paulson wore the refashioned coat-of-state with authority and charity. In peace the crofters and fishermen broke their furrows of clay and salt, and on small islands the long bright robes chanted their litanies; into which an expected name had not yet been gathered.

The story of Magnus and Hakon unfolds like a drama. Some day a play will be written about it; I have not the ability myself; but I end this chapter with a scene in dramatic form about an unrecorded cure at the tomb of Magnus, as a suggestion of what might be possible.

No saga-man would have written about folk like Jock and Mary, two vagrants who wander about the shores and burns, as secret and dangerous as otters.

Jock and Blind Mary are on the road, By hills, lochs, crofts, peatbogs, fishing boats, howes, hamlets, kirks, wells they go all the year round, from leaf-and-lamb, into the bronze of harvest, and into white winter, and, beyond it, into a new light.

MARY: What's at the end of this road?
JOCK: The Birsay kirk.
MARY: A kirk? What are we going to a kirk for? There's nothing to eat in a kirk. O no, I'm going to no kirk. I can assure you for that. Kirk indeed.
JOCK: Come on, then.

(*They trudge on.*)

MARY: I smell fish.
JOCK: The Hamnavoe boats. They're in from the west.

(*They arrive at Hamnavoe, a cluster of masts and grey houses at the edge of the shifting water.*
  Three fishermen with a net at a pier. They are putting their catch in separate boxes, uttering a slow chant.)

FIRST FISHERMAN: A fish for the king.

SECOND FISHERMAN: A fish for the kirk.

THIRD FISHERMAN: A fish for the earl.

FOURTH FISHERMAN: A fish for the laird.

MARY: A fish for the hungry.

FIRST FISHERMAN (*to Mary*): Watch out!

MARY: (*going deliberately among boxes, nets and fishermen's arms*):
A cod head for a poor blind wife. We have a long hard
way to go. My man's bad to me.

FIFTH FISHERMAN: Give her a crab, for God's sake. Get rid of
them.

(*The fishermen gave Mary a crab.*)

SIXTH FISHERMAN: A fish for the king.

SEVENTH FISHERMAN: A fish for the kirk.

FIRST FISHERMAN: A fish for the earl.

SEVENTH FISHERMAN: A fish for the laird.

THIRD FISHERMAN: A fish for the boat.

FOURTH FISHERMAN: A fish for the pot.

FIFTH FISHERMAN: A fish in the chimney smoke, for a winter
hunger.

(*Jock and Mary go on past the fishermen.*)

MARY: I got a hook in my finger. (*She sucks a drop of blood.*)
One small crab – the mean bastards.
(*To the crab.*) Don't snap your claw at me, hunchback,
(*To Jock.*) You take him. (*Jock puts the crab in his pocket.*)

(*They trudge on.*)

MARY: Ah, my poor feet!

JOCK: It's all right, We're half road there.

MARY: Where?

JOCK: The Birsay kirk.

MARY (*stopping*): I'm going to no Birsay kirk. You can go to
the Birsay kirk if you want to. Say Birsay kirk again and
I'll batter you – so help me God I will. Leave me at the

first ale-house door. (*They move on together.*) There'll be a time to go to the Birsay kirk, yes, and the Birsay kirkyard too, when we're cold and rotten.

(*They trudge on. The round hills of Stromness and Sandwick stand about them.*)

JOCK: Dark hills we're among, Miffia, Kringlafiold, Meeran-Bloo.

MARY (*cocking her head*): I hear a cluck-cluck-clucking in the ditch.

JOCK: A white chicken. (*He takes Mary by the arm and hurries her on.*) No more thieving. We're pilgrims. We need clean hands and clean hearts for the thing we're going to do today.

(*Mary shakes free from Jock. She makes coaxing noises, stooping down and beckoning with her finger. Then suddenly she jerks out her hand, grasps the chicken, and twists its neck.*)

MARY: There, sweetness. You won't be feared of the dog again. No, nor the hawk in the cloud either. (*She stows the chicken under her shawl.*)

JOCK: You've made a small snow-storm in the ditch. Hurry on. God forgive our thieving. (*He crosses himself.*)

(*They trudge on. Mary lags a little behind Jock, the breath harsh on her lip.*)

MARY: Jock.

JOCK: What now?

MARY: Don't go so fast. What's your hurry? Stop till I get my breath.

JOCK: We're going up Revay Hill, a steep place.

MARY (*she stops and listens*): What's Revay whispering about – whisper, whisper, whisper? I never heard such gossip.

JOCK: It's the scythe in the oats. The crofters are in the harvest field. A good crop too. Stooks as bright as trumpets.

(*They are climbing up Revay Hill, a heavy fertile wedge thrust into the surging blue and white of the sky.*

The farmer and his wife and hired harvesters are sitting in the shade of a wall eating their mid-day bannocks and cheese, and drinking ale. The scythes lean against the wall.)

MARY (*whining*): A bit of bread for an old blind wife. A bottle of ale to wash it down.

FARMER: Them bloody tinkers again! (*He shouts to his dog.*) Seize them, Bran! Take them, boy! See them off.

(*A dog barks among the oats. The farmer threatens Jock and Mary with his scythe.*)

JOCK (*backing off*): We're just going, I'm sorry sir. We won't trouble you at all. (*As the farmer still advances on him he produces a club from inside his coat.*) Only don't push me too far . . . (*In a panic.*) Do you see this club? You bloody ignorant yokel, don't thwart me, look at it, it's splashed red! It's scarlet with the blood of slaughtered men!

MARY (*screeching*): Crush him, Jock!

JOCK: I stood where thousands fell.

A HARVESTER: Was that the time you shook your shirt? (*The harvesters laugh.*)

FARMER (*advancing with raised scythe*): I'll cut you to ribbons, you trash!

THE FARMER'S WIFE (*coming between them: to her man*): Think shame. We were poor as them last winter. And poorer the winter before that. (*Her basket, brimming with food and flagons, is under the wall, in the shade. She takes a bannock and a bottle from it.*) The war's over. We can eat together in peace now, surely.

Remember this, we're only as rich as the poorest folk among us. (*She gives the bannock and ale to Mary.*)

MARY (*feeling the gift*): I've seen bigger rations in my time.

JOCK: Thank you, lady.

FARMER (*to the harvesters*): Come on. The whole field must be cut before dark.

THE HARVESTERS (*returning to their reaping with a chant*):
> Seven loaves –
> The laird gets one.
> The earl gets two.
> The king gets three.
> The seventh loaf,
> That's for the peasant.
> He must share it with God and the birds.

(*Jock and Mary trudge on.*)

MARY: It's cold all of a sudden.

JOCK: The sun's down.

MARY: Still, there's a good fire in the ale-house. It's the thought of that that's kept my feet going all day, the fire and the ale and somebody talking sense for a change.

(*An old soldier in the ditch, with an empty sleeve and a pin leg.*)

MARY (*holding her nose*): What a stink at the cross-roads!

JOCK: It's that old soldier with one arm and one leg.

SOLDIER: Please, a bite, friends.

MARY: Out of the way, you rag-bag.

SOLDIER: Pity, kind lady.

MARY: Don't 'kind lady' me. (*She feels his face with her hand.*) A bunch of thistles. What dung did the likes of you grow out of?

SOLDIER: I fought in the war, lady. The first winter I fought for Magnus. I was broken with horses' hooves – that's the way I lost my arm.

JOCK: And your leg's away too.

SOLDIER: An axe, sir. Just a bit of a scratch along the thigh. That was the second winter. I was on Hakon's side that

time. My leg turned purple. In the end they took it off
with a saw.

MARY: You won't do any more war dances. That's for sure.
I hope you're sorry. (*She spits.*) Bloody soldiers. I don't
give a damn about you. Come on, Jock.

SOLDIER: I'm hungry.

JOCK (*to Mary*): Give him a bit of bread.

MARY: No. The scum that he is. He'll think twice before he
puts on a helmet again.

JOCK (*offering the crab to the soldier*): Here then, take this.

MARY (*snatching the crab back and putting it under her shawl*):
Nothing for murderers.

(*They trudge on.*)

MARY: War's a good thing for blacksmiths.

JOCK: Yes, and girls and gravediggers.

MARY: I'm smelling the sea again.

JOCK: We're going down into Birsay.

MARY: There's a touch of silver in the air, a shiver.

JOCK: The moon's out over the village, a thin naked thing,
Mary, like a girl on her wedding night.

MARY: Listen to the old beast.

JOCK: I've watched the moon changing like a woman a
thousand times. I know all about the moon. First, this
trembling bride. Then a bee-wife with a honeycomb.
A few nights more and she's a red-faced washer-woman –
she swills linen in the burn, bright shirts. Then she's a
widow with a small candle.

MARY (*sarcastic*): Jock the poet.

JOCK: In the end she's nothing but an old bent hag, a poor
blind crone among the ashes. Then the black boards
nailed over her face . . . (*He crosses himself.*) Rack-curse-
cat-end-patchy.

MARY: So. (*She sighs.*)

(*They are approaching the steep green tidal holm of The Brough, with its cathedral and monastery and palace.*)

JOCK: Thank God the tide's out. We can cross over now.

MARY: Where are we?

JOCK: Never mind. Just hold on to the tail of my coat. We're on seaweed and slippery stones.

MARY (*her foot in a pool*): Ah!

JOCK: Don't yell like that. The holy brothers'll hear you. You put your foot in a pool, that's all. Come on.

MARY: The sea's on the one side of us and the sea's on the other side of us. We'll get drowned, Jock.

JOCK: The tide's far out. Listen, kittiwakes in the crag, all sleepy.

MARY: There's a seal splashing out there. Whistle to him.

JOCK: Quiet, We must be quiet.

MARY: Is there an ale-house the place we're going?

JOCK: No.

MARY (*screaming*): Ah – h–h–h!

JOCK: For God's sake! This is a place of silence.

MARY: I put my foot on a razor-fish. Are there any bits of toe on the rock? That slippery stuff's blood.

JOCK: It's seaweed. Take hold of my coat. Follow me. There's only one more pool . . . and a wet stone . . . and a few shells . . and sand . . . and now we're on the island. Be quiet. The Bishop doesn't like the kind of pilgrims he's getting lately. (*He listens.*) Come on.

MARY: Where to? I won't go a step further till I know where we're going.

JOCK: To the kirk.

MARY: I'M NOT GOING TO ANY KIRK.

JOCK: You must come.

MARY: I WILL NOT.

JOCK: Yes.

MARY: NO.

(*A pause.*)

MARY: I'm tired of the holy talk of them brothers every time they put a bandage on my eyes. *O my poor afflicted daughter, bear your cross with patience* . . . I don't want any more of that kind of talk. O no. I've had my belly-full of that palaver.

JOCK: Stay where you are, then. Sit on the beach. I won't be that long . . . (*He leaves Mary and goes up to the cathedral.*) I'll have to hurry before they start their Matins . . . (*He opens the heavy door cautiously, enters, dips his fingers in the holy water, crosses himself, genuflects to the altar, looks about him, and kneels down among the images, at a new tomb.*)

JOCK: Saint Magnus, are you hearing me? I made a tin pail for you in Rackwick last night. She sold it in a Hamnavoe pub for porter. Mary. She has a throat on her like a salt fish. Or more like a smouldering peat. Or more like a bit of the everlasting brimstone. Listen, Saint Magnus.

(*Silence. The muted sound of the sea, still ebbing.*)

Saint Magnus, I'll tell you what I'm here about, I won't hide it from you any longer. As if you didn't know my errand already. It's not me, it's that old woman.

(*Silence.*)

I've saved this bit of candle for you. (*He takes a candle from his pocket and lights it from one of the church candles and dribbles hot grease on the tomb and sets his offering up, a reeky flame.*) Beeswax. I'm trying hard to mind on a prayer. Light for light, Magnus. Ask the Lord to put a glimmer back in her skull.

MARY (*outside*): How much longer am I to bide out here in the cold!

JOCK: A small blink, Magnus. She was as shining a lass as ever walked the roads. You must have seen her in her best days, many a time, going to the Dounby Market with pans and laces, among the ponies and the fiddles and the tilting bottles. She could see in them days like a hawk through crystal.

MARY (*outside*): The ale's half done.

(*Silence.*)

JOCK: I'm not blaming you for not listening to a tink.

(*Silence.*)

She's nothing now. A mouth on her like a warped purse. Two cold stones for eyes. That's what Mary's come to. Just an old blind sack of sins.

MARY (*whimpering*): Jock, it's midnight. There's rats out here.

JOCK: All right, then, Magnus, say nothing. I was travelling through Birsay anyway, for rags. I just came in out of the wind for a minute. It isn't beeswax at all, this candle, it's whale tallow.

(*Silence.*)

I'll tell you what. I won't steal or swear any more. Tell the Lord God that. Truth, Magnus. No lies from now on. Every morning and every night I'll say the ten Hail Marys – beads of dew on a wild rose.

(*A thread of grey in the blackness of night.*)

MARY: JOCK.

(*Silence. The last glut of sea on a rock. It is full ebb.*)

JOCK: Well, well, say nothing. Maybe it's all for the best. Folk take more pity on a blind person, you get a lot more ha'pennies on the road, there's more to spend in the pub at the end of the day.

(More grey threads through the fabric of night, then a yellow thread . . . Jock turns to the sweetest statue in the cathedral.)

Our Lady of The Seven Sorrows . . .

(Bishop William enters.)

BISHOP: Who's that? . . . What are you wanting here? I couldn't sleep all night for the screaming of that old woman on the shore.

JOCK *(in a humble voice, struggling to his feet)*: Your reverence, I was asking the saint to help us.

BISHOP: The saint. What saint?

JOCK: Saint Magnus.

BISHOP: There's no Saint Magnus. You're wasting your time, my man. That's only the tomb of the earl who was murdered in Egilsay. You might as well pray to a stone. I'm getting a bit tired of telling that to all the poor things that come here. They're beginning to come now from as far away as Iceland and St Kilda – hare-lip and scab and consumption. Ugh!

JOCK: I'm sorry, your reverence.

BISHOP *(a little kinder)*: Whether this dead man is a saint or not is not for us to say. He might be. The authorities haven't decided yet. A man isn't a saint because all the tramps and tinkers of the day think he is. When Rome says he's a saint, that'll be time enough for me and you to ask for his help. Do you follow me?

JOCK: Yes, your reverence. Thank you.

(It is dawn. The small flame of Jock's candle is lost in widening circles of brightness.)

BISHOP: Bless your faith, all the same. The brothers are coming in to sing a litany, so you'd better go now. You had no business to be on this island at all, do you know that? This is private property.

JOCK: No, your reverence. Thank you. I won't come again.

(*The sea begins to turn round with a sound like a struck harp.*)

BISHOP: The old woman is quiet now – she's sleeping under the rock, I think. You can cook your breakfast. Then off with the pair of you.

JOCK: Yes, your reverence. Thank you. We'll do that.

BISHOP: I'll remember you both in my Mass.

(*Jock bows himself backwards out of the church. Bishop William shuts the door. The monks file into the choir with lit candles and censers swinging and voices going up and down.*)

MONKS: Kyrie eleison. Christe eleison. Kyrie eleison.

(*Mary wakens under the rock.*)

MARY (*yawning and stretching herself*): It's about time.

JOCK (*squatting down beside the fire on the beach: to Mary, very despondently*): That old twister, he drove me out of the holy church. Did you hear him?

MARY: We should get a bob or two for the candle-sticks. Did you pinch the chalice too?

JOCK: Shut up.

(*The monks begin to sing the Litany of the Saints of the North.*)

MONKS: *Saint Olaf the King, pray for us.*

JOCK: Is that all you left, the chicken neck?

MARY: I had the queerest dream. It was folk in a winter field, in the snow. They were all lamenting how poor they were. First was a merchant fat as a pig – one of his twelve ships was wrecked on Braga. A farmer then, girning – a rat was in his barn. Then a holy brother – 'O' cries he, 'I'm betrothed to the Lady Poverty' – and by God he looked it. Then – I never saw anything so queer – the King of Norway hung with silks and dia-

monds, he comes arm-in-arm with that old broken-
down soldier we passed yesterday on the road. They had
one bone between them and they were gnawing at it
like two dogs. Then they would leave off, and wail, and
throw their arms round each other. They all stood in
front of the kirk, and you were there in the kirk door,
Jock, you and the bishop and a man I didn't know.

JOCK: There was too much badness in you. The saint couldn't
do a thing.

MONKS: *Saint Ninian the traveller, pray for us.*

MARY: Then the birds wakened me . . . Jock, I'm hungry
again.

(*The sun had risen – the harvest sun – a vat of thick red
primeval clay, crammed with corn and ale for the bewintered
people of Orkney. Mary has been fashioned from the same
lovely clay – but now she is a worn-out begging-bowl. Today,
as every day, she knows that the pagan sun will give her a
bite and a sup. Vat and begging-bowl tilt, touch, pledge. The
sun is on her hands. Mary rises. She is ready for the road.*)

MARY: Jock, I said I'm hungry.

(*The sun has risen, lamp of the world. By its light men come
and go. Even at midnight, even in midwinter, the sun lends
a little oil for lantern, candle, taper. Mary's lamp has been
out this long time past. She knows better than to offer that
broken thing to the sun.*)

MARY: Come on. The sea's throwing her arms about the place.

(*Into the hands of every unborn soul is put a lump of the
original clay, for him to mould vessels – a bowl and a lamp –
the one to sustain him, the other to lighten him through the
twilight between two darknesses, birth and death. He refreshes
himself, this Everyman, with mortal bread; he holds his lamp
over rut and furrow and snow and stone, an uncertain flame.*

Now and then the honey of a hidden significance is infused into his being. By the vessels that he has moulded to his wants he calls this mystery of longing The – Immortal – Bread, The – Unquenchable – Light . . . At death he leaves behind the worn lamp and bowl, and (a peregrine spirit) seeks the table of the great Harvester, where all is radiance and laughter and feasting.

And some there are – God take pity on every soul born – that love their lamps and their bowls more than the source from which clay, corn and oil issue for ever; and, their vessels failing at last by reason of age or chance, they set out dark into the last Darkness, a drift of deathless wailing hungers . . .

The stump of Jock's candle reeks and sputters and goes out on the tomb.

A light that has once shone is never quenched. Can a diamond wither?

Harder than precious stones are acts of pity and praise and charity. The saints hoard them against our coming. With these jewels are purchased meantime many a miracle and blessing for the afflicted ones of the earth. Jock gets to his feet. A freshening wind throws the rising sea against The Brough. The smallest spume-drop is not lost – it is here, there, nowhere, everywhere, a frail blown cluster of salt bubbles; but also an emerald, an opal.)

MARY: Hurry on. I got spray on my face.

(Not the frailest thing in creation can ever be lost. A word, a smell, a flower, may be the hard rich symbol, recurring again and again in a man's life, by which we instantly recognise him; like the pattern of a few notes in a symphony. Spume on the psalter in a Welsh battle; the quenching in a rockpool of the terrible fires of lust; a cascade of spray over a hand steering a ship to an island – a single sea-drop wanders through a certain man's life, signing the supreme moments, a symbol and a leitmotif; as if the notes of his existence were to be purity and pain. Especially near the great moments salt water stings him –

99

war, love, death (and of course birth also, for besides the pure water of baptism a little salt is touched to the tongue).

This man is now in two places at once. He is lying with a terrible wound in his face, in the church near where the two tinkers are girding themselves for the road: The Brough, place of his beginning and end, birth and sepulchre. Also he is pure essence in another intensity, a hoarder of the treasures of charity and prayer, a guardian.

This fragrant vivid ghost is everywhere and always, but especially he haunts the island of his childhood. This morning he has been summoned by a candle, a small earth-to-heaven cry; its flame quickly quenched, and seemingly futile.

The wind goes through the Birsay corn in deep surges; whips crests from the Atlantic waves. The sea is coming in quickly, flushing out caves and crannies.

Saint Magnus the Martyr accepts the flame. He touches it to immortality, a hard diamond. The radiance he reserves, to give back again where it is needed.

A wave breaks on a rock near Jock and Mary and cascades them with spray, or with a squandered treasury of opal-and-pearl-and-emerald (it depends how you look at it).

The sources of Light are troubled for a moment.

A glister of oil spills into the quenched lamp.

Mary screeches. She puts her hands to her face.)

MARY: Ah-h-h-h! . . . A bird tore me!
JOCK: Nobody touched you.
MONKS: *Saint Tredwell, virgin, pray for us.*

(*Mary whimpers. Then she is quiet. She plucks, tremulously, a flower from the grass.*)

MARY: Daisies. (*She kneels.*) And here's a seapink.
JOCK: Don't torment me any more. I've had enough of you for one day.
MONKS: *Saint Cormac the sailor, pray for us.*

MARY (*getting to her feet, pointing*): That's a plover . . . There's a teeack.

JOCK (*stops eating and puts down his bone*): It's a lark, Mary.

MARY: That's what I said, a lark. I know a lark when I see one. (*She looks at Jock.*) What's this, like a rat's face?

JOCK: It's me you're looking at, Mary.

(*A pause.*)

MARY: We must be making do with what we have. You had black hair last time I saw you. (*She plucks a hair out of her own head and looks at it and gives it to the wind.*) God keep me from pools. God keep me from stones that shine in the rain . . . Jock, will there be stars tonight? (*She licks her finger and holds it up.*) I thought the wind was yellow at this time of year, harvest. (*She begins to move off.*) There's a lot of places I want to see, the Birsay ale-house for one. It's sure to be open by this time . . . (*She bends over the grass till her face shines like a woman at a milk-churn.*) Buttercups. That was a good name to give them. (*She wanders off.*) The stones are awash. All right then, I'll find my own way across.

(*Mary goes out.*)

JOCK: Who would think a ha'penny candle would light up the world?

(*The great red clay is clear of the hills now.*)

MONKS: *Saint Columba of the islands, pray for us.*

(*Jock stamps out the fire. He goes up to the door of the church.*)

JOCK: *Saint Magnus the Martyr, pray for us* . . . Jock the tinker said it before any of you.

(*He takes his bundle in his hand and moves off after Mary.*)

CRUSADER

In the years 1149 and 1150 the shipyards of western Norway rang with the noise of hammer on nails, rasped with saws. Fifteen large ships were being built for a Viking crusade; one in particular was a magnificent vessel – 'she had thirty-five thwarts, a great piece of craftsmanship, ornamented overall, figurehead and poop and weather-cocks gold-inlaid, carved entirely from stem to stern' . . . She was being built to the order of Rognvald Kolson, Earl of Orkney.

Rognvald Kolson was nephew to the martyred Magnus. He is the most attractive person in the Saga of the Orkney-men – soldier, statesman, poet, lover, adventurer. He had initiated the building of the Cathedral church of Saint Magnus in 1137. While the itinerant masons were busy in Kirkwall with the blocks of grey and red stone, the Earl travelled between Orkney and Norway to see to the building of his ship. Both these works – ship and church – bore witness to his obsession with the guilt of the Norsemen: their hawkflight through the history of Europe, blood-dripping beak and claw, the murder, piracy, rape, war, sacrilege perpetrated on the coasts of England, Ireland, France, even as far as Greenland

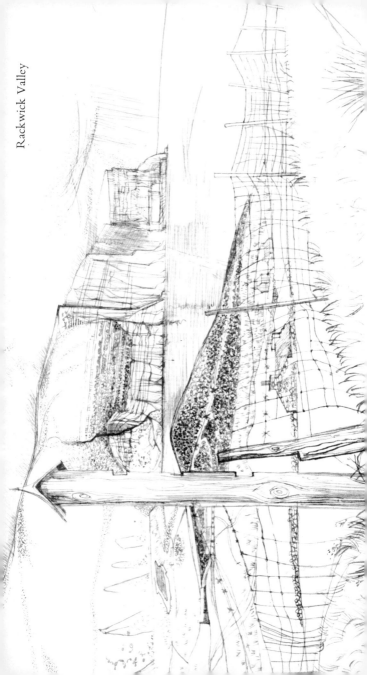

Rackwick Valley

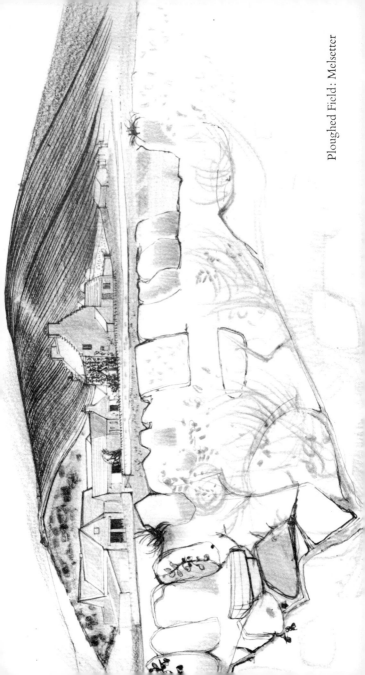

Ploughed Field: Melsetter

Old Houses Stromness

St. Magnus Church: Egilsay

West Pier: Kirkwall

The Ross Puma ashore in Hoy

and the Volga. These trespasses were now to be cancelled out. A penitential voyage to the Holy Land seemed one way of redeeming the cruel history of the north.

So the shipyards of Norway rang with hammers and rasped with saws and shrieked with adzes for two winters.

But a ship is a fragile thing, a migrant, her flight quickly over. In Kirkwall the master-mason consulted his plan and the labourers levered the ponderous blocks of stone. Only the foundations were dug as yet. This unmoving Cathedral church would take hundreds of years to build; its voyage was through history; the long nave was Christ-orientated like the brief ships. Its freight was a few bones and a cloven skull (the martyr's relics) and the bread and wine renewed daily on the altars, and the thousands of souls who would voyage God-wards, generation by generation, out of Orkney.

Earl Rognvald chose some of the finest men in Norway to accompany him on the voyage – Erling Ormson, Aslak Erlendson, Magnus Havardson, Sweyn Roldson, John Peterson, Thorbjorn Black. There was also a man called Eindred. Eindred was essential to the success of the crusade. It was Eindred who had sown the idea in the Earl's mind. He had sailed that way before; for a time he had been an officer of the Varangi, the Scandinavian guard of the Emperor at Byzantium. The man was brave, reckless, greedy. He built his own ship secretly, and in secret covered the hull with gold; of the fifteen crusading ships it had been agreed that only Earl Rognvald's was to have that aureate splendour.

Also in the ships was a group of Iceland poets, Ubi, Oddi, Armod. They were glad to leave their volcanoes and glaciers and tight-fisted patrons for a year or two. On the voyage they knew they would be treated generously, for Earl Rognvald was himself one of the best skalds of the north.

Also in the company was the Bishop of Orkney, William, 'a clerk of Paris,' an old man now but ruddy and thick and strong, and a few of his chaplains.

The fleet wintered in Orkney. The crews, Norwegians and Orkneymen, did not get on well with each other; knives glinted in the ale-houses; there were bloody noses and bruised fists at the Kirkwall street corners; a corpse in the seaweed. One company of seamen broke into Maeshowe, the huge Stone Age Burial chamber, through the roof. (This was a flourish of bravado, a piece of derring-do; earlier desecrators of the tomb, innocent shelterers from a snow storm, had been driven mad by the ghostly guardians of the treasure.) The pilgrims found no gold or ivory; the tombs had been rifled long before; but they covered the walls with runes to let everyone know they had been that way – *Ingibiorg is the most beautiful of the women . . . Hermund carved these runes with a hard axe . . . Many a lovely lady, low stooping, has passed this way . . .*

The ships sailed from Scapa into the North Sea in the late summer of 1151, after the Orkneymen had cut their corn. The Iceland poets made lyric after lyric as the ships beat south.

> Wave and spindrift
> Higher than the mast.
> Over there is the Humber
> And a low coast.
> Hug the fire, clod-hopper.
> Ride home, councillor,
> With dry boots.

The passage through the Straits of Gibraltar was very stormy. Among the noises of wind and sea the thin harps sounded.

> Three happy days I remember,
> The ride on the mountain,

Then ale and talk
Beside a fire in the castle.
– Not these hogsheads of salt
Splashing our shields.
The Earl spurs the ship,
A grey stallion,
Between Europe and Africa.

Soon they were in the Mediterranean, undulating acres of blue silk. A dangerous sea: the Sirens had sung across these waters and Circe in her island had turned men into swine – the Bishop, who knew the classics, did not omit to remind the sailors of these things.

Their first landfall was the seaport of Narbonne in southern France. It is doubtful if the sight of so many Norse ships in the harbour roused any enthusiasm among the senators of the town; they reminded each other of what the Danes had done in Paris, and drew their hands across their throats. The merchants, however, spread flagons and trinkets and holy relics in front of their booths; sailors were good spenders. The young women of any port in the world at any time dance and clap their hands when foreign ships anchor in the bay. The coastguards measured the sea with indifferent eyes. In the monastery the calm voices went on with their plainchant – the same voices that, less than a century before, had sent up a new anguished appeal to God: *A furore Normanorum, libera nos, Domine.*

Earl Rognvald went ashore to pay a formal courtesy call on the prince of the city; who turned out to be a young beautiful woman, the Countess Ermengarde.

In his veins it was suddenly April. Birds sang. A rose budded.

Up to that time Earl Rognvald had known no women but

the cold strong women of the north, whose actions were a long ritual played out in twilight and secrecy. In the day-time their tasks cloistered them, kept them indoors from the world's stir. Men went about their ploughing, fishing, trading, adventuring under the broad sun. These women had a stony patience that men found fascinating and frightening. They were the sea watchers; they stood at the rock before dawn, after sunset, whenever the ships and the fishing boats were out, their eyes cold as kittiwakes. They hovered like priest-esses about the mysteries of birth and love and death, swaddling the infant, shrouding the corpse, permitting men to lie with them in the fecund darkness so that a new generation of providers might inherit the islands. Their instincts told them, too, that a family is only strong and thrusting so long as it is locked in dangerous conflict with the farmers over the hill, with the seaport along the coast, with the neighbouring kingdom. The secret promptings of women are behind much of the heroism and tragedy of the Iceland sagas . . . In such circumstances love is a bitter honey.

Here in France the mystery was suddenly sweet and fragrant, an opening rose.

That night the Earl made a new poem.

> Golden one,
> Tall one,
> Moving in perfume and onyx,
> Witty one,
> You with the shoulders
> Lapped in long silken hair.
> Listen: because of me
> The eagle has a red claw.

Earl Rognvald and the Countess Ermengarde celebrated the Romance of the Rose all that summer in Narbonne. The sailors were bemused with novelty too – black-haired girls in the whorehouses, white wine in the taverns – they swilled the sweet piss till they were sick. Armod and Ubi and Oddi discussed metre and rhyme with the Provençal troubadours; they listened amazed to the Mediterranean lyrics, 'roses and love and nightingales,' a dulcet intricate patterning, stanza after stanza. When Armod recited heroic lays to them, *Jomsvikings*, *The Everlasting Battle*, Messer Marcabrun and Bernard of Ventadour picked up their lutes and went away, smiling. And in the ornate churches the old Bishop listened while the priests celebrated Masses according to some rich Provençal rite.

With great difficulty they tore themselves from the silken webs of Narbonne. Armod made a poem about the departure.

> Now beauty is something other.
> Throw, voyagers,
> A last farewell to Ermengarde.
> (All them cut-throats
> As well as Armod
> Had one wild dream,
> To snore in her bed.)
> O heart-broken poet –
> That gold-and-ivory brow!

They arrived at the Spanish coast before Christmas.

The cooks announced that the Yule dinner would be like a dinner in Lent: the ships' larders were bare of sirloins, the wine barrels were empty. The crusaders bargained in a coast village for beef and bread and drink; they rattled the money bags. 'What's the good of silver to us?' said the village chief to Earl Rognvald, and shook his fist at a round strong building in the foot-hills. 'Godfrey and his soldiers and his tax-men come out of that castle whenever we cut our corn, whenever the fishing boats come in, and they wring us dry, I'll tell you what, you destroy that castle and we'll provide you with as many stores as you need, and for as long as you like . . .' The Earl and the captains agreed. It was time for them to do a bit of fighting – the silks and wine-skins of Narbonne had softened them. Besides, this would not be Viking marauding, it was war appropriate to their new status as Christian knights. They were to lift up the poor and humble and put down the mighty from their seats. They surveyed the castle, sharpened their axes, made plans for the assault.

By the time the ladders and battering-rams were brought up it was the vigil of Christmas, and the Bishop strictly forbade any fighting for the next twelve days. They celebrated Christmas meekly, hearing Mass daily and eating iron rations. Every night among the camp fires they discussed the impending assault. An old Spaniard in rags moved about among the groups of men, getting an occasional bone to gnaw with the dogs. This scarecrow (though the Norsemen did not know it) was the castellan, the lord Godfrey of the Knights of Castile. The beggar-lord saw, soon enough, that there was serious dissension among the crusaders, and that the disruptive faction was led by Eindred. Eindred and the mendicant had long conversations among the broken lights and shadows.

The morning after Twelfth Night the assault began. The Norse captains and their men, wedge on wedge of steel, stood all round the castle. The assault troops advanced with shouts of *The Lady Ermengarde!* and *Saint Magnus the Martyr!* and set ladders against the wall. The defenders poured down smoking tar and stones on the domed helmets. Archers from the battlement strung their bows, and the rapturous quivering birds carried this Shetland crofter and that Faroese fisherman to Valhalla or Purgatory, nobody knew quite where in all the yelling and confusion.

These breakers of steel and stone fell against the castle all morning.

Erling Ormson, who was the best strategist among the Norsemen, saw that up to now the assault was a failure. He had been poking his finger into the binding between the stones of the castle. He came back to the Earl and told him that the cement was made from a very poor quality lime; it would not be able to stand up to fire.

The Earl ordered logs and brushwood and all kinds of kindling to be brought up and piled against the base of the wall. The villagers ran from their hearths with blazing torches.

In the heart of the battle Earl Rognvald had time for poetry.

> White as snow,
> White as silver,
> The Lady,
> A beauty all whiteness,
> A kindness
> Red as wine.
> Another redness, fire
> About the castle,
> A sharp whiteness, swords.

Godfrey stood on the castle battlement and turned north and gravely saluted. Eindred and his Norwegians had been stationed there all morning, waiting to move in whenever the breach was made. Eindred raised his hand in reply. A stiff cold breeze was blowing from the south.

Torches were thrust into brushwood. The castle stood rooted in fire. The villagers ran back and fore for an hour with logs. The tide of flame lapped higher. Village dogs ran yelping from showers of sparks. A great crack ripped across the wall of the castle. Women shrieked inside. Earl Rognvald spoke to the village chief. No more kindling was needed; they should bring buckets of water instead. A splashing chain of villagers and seamen formed between the well and the castle.

Earl Rognvald signalled to his captains that the time for the final assault was near. Some of the Norsemen began to work themselves into a frenzy. They pranced and howled. They tore off their leather shirts. They bit the edges of their shields. They beat on their naked chests and shrieked till their mouths foamed like new-filled horns of ale.

Deluges of water were thrown on the hot stones of the castle. The steam mingled with the smoke from the fires and a dense fog rolled slowly northwards on the wind. Eindred and his phalanx stood like ghosts at their appointed station.

Sigmund remembered his sweetheart in Orkney.

> Seek her out, birds.
> In April tell this
> To Sigmund's girl.
> (In quiet islands
> She turns her wheel.)
> *At dawn young Sigmund*
> *Went before heroes*
> *And captains*
> *Under a battlement*
> *When the red wheel of war was turning.*

A horn was blown. The battering rams moved in. The stones in the wall tottered and fell like a collapsing sea. Against the breach moved the besiegers; into the interior of the castle that was as hot now as a bakehouse; into a brief last clash of swords, into the rape and the killing and the loot . . .

The sagaman does not say what the Bishop thought of his Christian knights that day. They had behaved no better than their grandfathers, the blond Viking beasts – worse, because the crusaders wore the masks of Christianity. This action at the castle, coming after the whoring and wine-bibbing at Narbonne, cast a dubious light on the pilgrimage. Besides, life and society being so complex, even in the twelfth century, the Norsemen would never know how the destruction of the castle might affect all that part of Spain. In the castle were kept, perhaps, the law-book, the music, the hawk, the tapestry, the chronicles, the swords and palms of civil peace; because of the castle the bandits stayed in the mountains and each man in the village did his appointed work. The Norsemen had listened to a few anarchists and now the culture and economy of the region might well have been destroyed, and after they had sailed away eastwards, chaos would come again.

There were corpses everywhere in the smoking rubble, churned up and hardly recognisable; but the villagers, turning over cold limbs and faces, recognised the taxman and the chaplain and the poet (Armod examined for a long time his broken viol), the executioner, the lawyer, the falconer, the hand-maidens, the horsemen. But where was the castellan himself? There was no sign of the lord Godfrey of the Knights of Castile, though they removed stone from stone and rooted in cellar and dungeon till darkness fell. The tyrant had melted into the smoke. The Norsemen returned to the ships with red hands and blackened faces. The villagers carried aboard salted geese, hogsheads of wine, loaves by the hundred, enormous cheeses, haunches of oxen, and tripes and sausages and onions and olives and grapes by the barrel.

The crusaders ate their Yule dinner late that winter.

In the morning they were seaborne again; and the Earl dedicated all his victories, past and future, to the golden-haired woman of Narbonne.

> The small mouth of Ermengarde
> Commands two things –
> A sea strewn with wreckage
> As far as Jordan,
> And later, in autumn
> With other migrant wings
> A returned prow.

*

Off Sardinia the helmsman sighted, between blocks of sea fog, two steep islands. The fog swirled round the islands and hid them again. The helmsman informed the Earl and his captains. Rognvald looked at his chart; no stacks or holms were indicated as being at that particular place; but the chart was a crude affair, mostly guesswork and fable. The fog came down thicker than ever; the dragon prow was a ghost; sea and sky one grey heave, and the mysterious islands lost.

There were only ten ships in the crusade. In the double obscurity of night and fog Eindred and five other captains had parted company from the main fleet. On the whole Earl Rognvald was relieved; Eindred had been an embarrassment ever since the building of the ships in Norway. He had covered his own ship in gold (only the Earl's ship was to have such adornment). He had tried consistently to outsail the Earl in the North Sea, as if the pilgrimage were some kind of a race. In Orkney and Narbonne Eindred's sailors were mixed up in every tavern brawl. After the capture of the Spanish castle he wore Godfrey's opals and emeralds on his fingers, so that there was no doubt in anybody's mind as to his duplicity in the matter of Godfrey's escape.

Earl Rognvald and his captains were glad to be quit of such a guide; they would find their own way; the blind ships groped eastwards through the windless shrouds and prisms of fog. To the north, towards Sardinia, the fog shredded thin again as the Earl wrinkled his brow over the charts. Where the two steep islands had been there stood now, against a scrape of blue sky, only one island, an island with a spread of huge sails.

'That,' said Earl Rognvald, 'must be the biggest ship in the world . . .' The second island-ship was lost in a thicker clot of fog.

In a sea that swarmed with Moroccan and Barbary and Corsican pirates, the Egyptian merchants built their dromonds – freighted with pearls and lions and corn and alligator skins for Italy – as superb and massive as swans among the small fowl of the coasts. Any hawk did well to falter and turn away from such power.

There seemed to be small point in the Norsemen attacking her either. They could do with some plunder; they had squandered silver like rain in France; in Spain their Epiphany provisions had cost them a fortune. It looked as though they might have to borrow heavily from the Jews in Acre if they were to make any kind of showing at all in Jerusalem and Byzantium and Rome. But the immense curves of the ship, as they came on her suddenly out of the fog, daunted them. Too many sailors would die in the onset, scalded with tar and sliced with scimitars; and, with their depleted numbers, they could not spare one pilgrim more.

The dark sailors greeted their approach with a carnival display. They spread silken webs and bales along the hull, whether as a taunt or as a bribe the Norsemen could not tell, but it tormented them with a hint of enormous wealth in the holds.

If she had been a Christian merchant ship they could not, as pilgrims, have attacked her. To destroy an infidel seemed, on the other hand, to be a positive duty, quite apart from any prospect of loot. But all they could do was make a gesture – stand off and sting the Saracen with a flight of arrows, then regroup and sail on eastwards; the prows before them like fingers touched in prayer.

Erling Ormson, after standing for a long time with head tilted on fist (by the end of the day he was to go for ever with his head askew, like a wise bird) said that in his opinion it was possible to board the dromond. In this way: four ships would sail in quickly and hug the dromond close, two on the port side and two on the starboard side. The swelling curve of the hull was a positive advantage to them, because the hot tar and missiles thrown down by the infidels would go into the sea – well, a spatter or two might scald a Norse head, to prevent which, the outside rowers must hold up their shields like wide hats. 'Then,' said Erling Ormson, 'we simply hack our way into the dromond with axes, tear a door through the side of her . . .' There would be hand-to-hand fighting in the gloom of the lower deck; then, as more and more Norsemen poured in, the negroes would retreat up to the top deck, if only to see better what they were doing; there they would be met by flight on flight of arrows from the other Norse ships standing a little way off. A favourable outcome, in Erling Ormson's opinion, seemed likely.

Earl Rognvald ordered the men to arm themselves.

The battle went like a song. Iceland poets and Shetland fishermen had never seen negroes before; all they knew, in the trance of battle, was that negroes' blood was red like their own and that they felt pain, and Thorfinn the Stronsay crofter saw that when a youth in a turban had his arm cut off another grey-bearded negro wept over him and tried to comfort him and at last, in a thicket of axes, blessed his dying. Thorfinn supposed that it didn't matter so much about negroes, they were infidels and they were bound for hell anyway, but this and that small facet of the battle moved him to pity. He saw that bravery and grief are common to all men, blond and black, Christian and Moslem.

By late afternoon the dromond resembled a slaughterhouse. Almost the entire ship's company was dead except the captain and a few others; the captain was being held, a prisoner, on board the Bishop's ship.

The search for loot was a frantic disappointment; hardly anything of value was found – a few turbans, hookahs, bloodstained cloths. The dromond was in ballast. She was obviously bound home, having unloaded her cargo at Naples or Marseilles . . . And yet, Earl Rognvald reasoned with his captains, Egyptian merchants don't give away their treasures for nothing. Somewhere in the broken ship was a chest full of coin of Lombardy.

He had the Negro captain brought into his cabin. The man had been shockingly maltreated; his face was bruised and blood-caked, one eye was half-closed, his arms were raw from the ropes that still held him. The Norsemen kicked him into the cabin like an ox into a shambles. Earl Rognvald ordered him to be untied. The man said nothing. Earl Rognvald told him that he was a prisoner of Christian knights who were making a holy voyage to the source of their religion. The negro said nothing. Speaking courteously and urbanely, with a glint of humour here and there, Earl Rognvald told him what had happened in Biscay and France and Spain; he mentioned Ermengarde and Godfrey and Eindred; such adventures, he said, though delectable, cost a great deal of money (as his guest would appreciate), especially the galanterie in Narbonne, the wine and the roses. He paused, and smiled. The negro's head was a block of ebony.

'Now please tell me,' said the Earl quietly, 'where your money chest is.'

The black man said nothing.

Erling was standing at the table. He had a bloody bandage round his neck. His battle wound would give the head of that wise councillor a pensive cast for ever. It had just earned him a new name. He was no longer Erling Ormson, walking the world simply by virtue of being the fruit of his father's loins. From this day on he was the wise old bird, the branded warrior, he was Erling Twistneck.

Earl Rognvald turned to Twistneck and ordered the dromond to be set on fire and cut adrift. Tar barrels were broken, torches thrown into the ship, cables severed. The dromond drifted away into the fog with her dead men. Suddenly she shook out into crimson flame, a spectral sea-rose, and drifted further away, dropping red petals into the Mediterranean. While the Norsemen watched, through the blackened hull flowed streams of molten gold and silver into the sea.

The negro skipper put his hands to his face and wept.

That night in the ships a dispute flared as to who had been the first man aboard the dromond. Various names were canvassed, only to be sneered at and shouted down. It was a matter of the greatest importance for this question to be settled at once, so that there was no blurring of history. Every battle-account must have its outstanding hero; this was a hallowed convention. A clash of versions would cast a doubt on the entire venture when they got home again: farmers in Birsay and merchants in Trondheim would say, winking to each other over a winter fire, that perhaps they had made up the story of the dromond, and botched it into the bargain, in the taverns of Narbonne – it was impossible for so many eagles to exist on the same mountain . . . Who, then, was the one hero of the sea-battle? Names were mentioned only to be howled down and derided. Finally they appealed to Earl Rognvald.

Earl Rognvald said,

> Audun the Red
> Was the earliest reaper
> In this harvest
> Black sheaves
> Fell on the dromond.
> Flame-bearded Audun
> Was all gules.
> Erling's Audun
> Through fire and blood
> Bound his red harvest.

Everybody agreed at once that Audun from Erling's ship was the first man on board the dromond, the outstanding hero, prince of the battle and the story.

Poetry, besides being a dancer, sets its laurel on the head of truth.

The ten crusading ships turned south-east, taking the negro merchant to his home port in Africa. For the rest of the voyage

116

he and Earl Rognvald treated each other like friends, eating at the same table, conversing easily and openly.

They sat together over their last breakfast in the harbour. The negro drank water with his bread; Earl Rognvald had his cup of wine.

What did they speak about? Only one piece of conversation is recorded. The negro thanked the Earl 'for having spared my life and treated me with as much honour as you know how. But I would be glad enough if we never saw each other again. Now all health and happiness to you . . .'

He went ashore then, a ruined merchant, and was lost among the tumultuous black faces of the seaport.

On watch off Crete one stormy night, Armod thought about his Iceland girl. Before dawn he had a new poem.

> Night. Sheets of salt.
> Armod on watch.
> A heave and wash of lights from the island.
> The lads of Crete
> Toss in hot tumbled linen.
> This poet on watch
> Cold, burning, unkissed.

In the harbour of Acre plague broke out in some ships. Many of the Norsemen died. Sailor after sailor was dumped overboard. Thorbjorn Black died, but he was a captain and so he was carried into the church and buried there. Oddi spoke his elegy.

> Bear him, sailors,
> Thorbjorn with the black beard.
> Bear gently, poets,
> The harp of Thorbjorn.
> Carry with candles

The king's friend
Deep in the vaults of the kirk.
Requiem aeternam da ei.
Southern stones,
Pile over Thorbjorn Black a bright howe.

Earl and Bishop and captains rode on hired horses to Jerusalem. In the Church of the Holy Sepulchre they went slowly along the fourteen painted Stations of the Cross, following Christ – the one painful broken death-going that redeems the multitudinous trespasses of mankind, lost in the huge waste between Eden and Paradise.

They were sailors. They saw the *Via Crucis* in terms of a ship on the sea. The whole world was a vessel voyaging through space and time, both free and fated, and Christ the Hero a captain-captive.

| I | JESUS IS CONDEMNED | The young Hero steps on board his ship. The death voyage begins. Soldiers stand all about him, a steel vigil. |

(*The Norsemen knelt. They said* Pater Noster. *They said* Ave Maria. *They said* Gloria. *They rose to their feet.*)

| II | JESUS IS MADE TO BEAR HIS CROSS | A sail goes up with a cross on it (as if this ship were to be stroked out, cancelled). Beyond the headland, a wind strikes the death ship. The Hero stands at the helm. |

(Pater Noster. Ave Maria. Gloria.)

| III | JESUS FALLS FOR THE FIRST TIME | Darkness. The gale tears the helm from the Hero's fist. The death ship rolls among the waves. The soldiers drag the Hero to his feet. |

(Pater Noster. Ave Maria. Gloria.)

IV   JESUS MEETS   The darkness is riven. A planet, Star
      HIS MOTHER   of the Sea, lights the Hero's path for
                           an hour, an illumination piercing
                           and pure.

(Pater Noster. Ave Maria. Gloria.)

V   SIMON HELPS   A man from the rowing benches,
     JESUS TO   with thick shoulders, takes the helm
     CARRY HIS   from the storm-broached Hero, at
     CROSS   behest of the soldiers.

(Pater Noster. Ave Maria. Gloria.)

VI   VERONICA   They shelter in a bay. The Hero steps
      WIPES THE   ashore. A croft girl wipes sweat and
      FACE OF   salt and blood – a mask of carnage –
      JESUS   from the Hero's face, most tenderly,
                  with a new cloth from the loom.

(Pater Noster. Ave Maria. Gloria.)

VII   JESUS FALLS   The ship clears the headland. The
      FOR THE   Hero navigates. Terrible the storm
      SECOND TIME about the helm – about faltering
                  Hero and fallen Hero and Hero flung
                  to his feet once more.

(Pater Noster. Ave Maria. Gloria.)

VIII JESUS SPEAKS At the shore of the Island of Women,
      TO THE   much lamentation (and ever will be)
      DAUGHTERS OF for fisherman and sailor, for sea loss
      JERUSALEM   and stark shapes in the sand, and
                  especially for this death-bound
                  skipper, the Hero (it had been
                  promised them) that would rescue

their island from the Dragon of hunger and loss.

(Pater Noster. Ave Maria. Gloria.)

IX JESUS FALLS FOR THE THIRD TIME

The Hero has fallen on deck a third time. No Hero rises. Blood-and-Salt-and-Thorns is dragged to its feet by the soldiers.

(Pater Noster. Ave Maria, Gloria.)

X JESUS IS STRIPPED OF HIS GARMENTS

And Nakedness is thrust at the helm. There is no shame or mockery they will not put on him, the soldiers. They have made him, in that Dragon-wake, barer than beast. Red from lash and seaweed, the Hero flings from a sudden rasp of rock!

(Pater Noster. Ave Maria. Gloria.)

XI JESUS IS NAILED TO THE CROSS

The ship is broken under the Hero. The waters of the end are all about him.

(Pater Noster. Ave Maria. Gloria.)

XII JESUE DIES ON THE CROSS

The waters come in even unto his soul. Salt blocks his throat.

(Pater Noster. Ave Maria. Gloria.)

XIII JESUS IS TAKEN DOWN FROM THE CROSS

The Hero is cast ashore on the Island of Women. Three dark shawls at the rock, after sunset. A heavy shadow lifted from a wash and glim of surf. A loud gull cry. And the face of the

woman who holds the Hero bright
as a star.

(Pater Noster. Ave Maria. Gloria.)

XIV JESUS IS   Fishermen lower the Hero into his
    PLACED IN   shore grave. From shore to shore of
    THE   the world the Dragon walks. The
    SEPULCHRE   voyage is over.

(Pater Noster. Ave Maria. Gloria.)

Fourteen pictures along three walls; but for their genuflec-
tions, one might think they were visitors in a gallery looking
at art. They are not looking *at* anything; they are looking into
the fourteen mirrors that show God's love of men, and men's
answer to God – not static pictures, but a moving glimmer
and brilliance and darkness; time and space reflected infinitely
in every direction; the very Face that brooded on chaos
among, now, their own proud lascivious cruel greedy faces.
In those fourteen terrible mirrors they glimpse themselves.
The image changes from water to fire. Rognvald, Erling,
John Peterson, Aslak, Solmund, Audun strut, a moving hedge
of steel, under a torment of sun, along the Jerusalem – Gol-
gotha road. They are the bearers of the lash, the parchment,
the dice, the thorns, the nails, the hammer, the lance. On they
clash. In the forge of his passion The Word will transform
these terrible instruments into a chalice, and, of his endless
courtesy, give it back to them. On they clash, and on, and into
the red-dappled smithy.

The pain of the mirrors has flung the pilgrims down
fourteen times. They are long in rising from the Station of the
Tomb. They have repented a sin or two many times, in
confessional and bed-closet; now, here, at last, for ever, they
will passionately that their whole cruel history – its symbol
the dragon-headed Viking longship – might be drowned and
buried with the dead Christ.

They cross themselves. They rise with difficulty from the fourteenth station. They turn. The open door of the church is before them, a silver murmuring arch: the unresolved fifteenth station. They leave the church, they are gathered into the life of the streets and the seafront; all the viciousness, vanity, lust, that have been and will be again. But on behalf of a whole people they have confessed, they have been shriven, they have done their penance, a dove out of the storm has fallen on them. They move through the door – the fifteenth mirror, where all is glimpsed darkly – into (for however long) the light of grace; towards another keel, new masts, a more perfect voyage.

Between Acre and Byzantium Earl Rognvald composed a poem.

> We have left the share to rust
> In a northern field,
> Exchanged oxen for sea horses.
> We make salt furrows
> As far as Byzantium.
> We will be the Emperor's husbandmen,
> Winnowing chaff from the holy grain.
> May we be worthy at last
> For the glory of Christ the King
> To break bread in the white churches.

The ships stayed for most of a winter in the harbour of Byzantium. Earl Rognvald and the Norse captains were well received by the Emperor Manuel. He offered them commissions in his Scandinavian guard, the Varangi. The Earl begged to be excused. He was deeply impressed by all that he had seen in the eastern capital – white domes, jade wine cups, the olive-skinned Greek girls, the ikons, Arab mathematicians, Persian poets, ships from Ceylon, the mosaics (especially one huge mosaic that covered a palace wall – The Risen Christ – each small stone dug from scattered quarries of the east, a white flame or a red flame or a yellow flame raised out of darkness and set by the artist in the order of resurrection, as if the elements too are renewed in Christ); but his people in their few barren Atlantic islands had been without their lord for nearly three years. God knows what evil – famine, pestilence, usurpation – might have happened to them in the meantime. He thanked the Emperor for his generosity, but as soon as his ships were provisioned from His Majesty's granaries and dockside store-houses, they must sail into the sunset and through the Pillars of Hercules. The Emperor smiled; assented; the peacock fans fluttered; the imperial chair was uplifted, borne away.

Under an arch stood the traitor Eindred, a captain in the guard of the Varangi once more, unsmiling, his sword erect before him and dividing his face in two.

The Earl returned to Orkney, by way of Rome and Denmark and Norway. His pilgrimage had lasted almost three years, a long and hard time for his people. He had much trouble to unravel, many things to put to rights, before the islands were at peace again.

The itinerant masons were still at work in Kirkwall. Slowly the cathedral Church of Saint Magnus the Martyr, a new ark, a great stone ship, rose from the dragon-head they had sunk through the waters of penance, in Jerusalem. The crusaders – home once more – stood in a nave the colour of agony. This church must carry the people of Orkney across many centuries – seas of tranquillity and rage and apathy – the years flashing and falling from her bow like cloven waves, towards the City of God.

4

LORE

THE MIDSUMMER MUSIC

THE MIDWINTER MUSIC

THE MIDSUMMER MUSIC

In Ornkey, one summer midnight, two fiddlers were walking home together from a wedding. In a field at the roadside was a mound – a howe, a knoll, a knowe – one of those artificial green humps that we now know to be burial chambers of the neolithic people. One of the fiddlers turned to answer his companion's half-finished sentence. He was not there. The lonely fiddler on the road knew then that the other fiddler had been taken down into the darkness. He was entombed, alive and enchanted, in the howe.

Some time later – none of the legends agrees as to exactly how long; some say a year, some ten years, some forty years – the unenchanted fiddler was walking along that same road with the knowe at the verge of it when he heard a lithe step beside him. He turned and saw that the howe-taken fiddler was once more on the road, walking home with him, his fiddle in his hand, in his mouth the end of the sentence he had not managed to complete. He was not an hour older than the day he disappeared, his beard was still black and curly and his eye bright. But time had happened to the workaday fiddler; there was grey in his hair and labour had worn his hands closer to the brightness of the bone.

On they walked together.

It is perhaps an attempt to explain what used to be called 'the timeless quality' of art. But the myth goes deeper than that; it shows how, in the minds of the peasantry, art is interwoven with death and fruition. The fiddle, the skull, and the cornstalk yield their full significance only when they are seen in relation to each other.

The fiddler had been stolen by the earth people; not by the winter trows, who are all famine and deformity, but by the good trows, the potent energies of the earth that quicken grass and corn. They had stolen the fiddle so that its music would make the corn tall and golden under the sun that summer.

(It is interesting to know that the parents of Washington Irving belonged to the island of Shapinsay in Orkney. His story *Rip Van Winkle* shifts the Orkney folk tale to an American setting. *Rip Van Winkle* is an accomplished but rootless story – the power and urgency and meaning of the myth have vanished.)

In the centre of Orkney, between the two lochs of Stenness and Harray, on a stretch of moor, stands the Ring of Brodgar – a circle of huge monoliths. We will never know what kind of neolithic ceremonies – hymn and procession and sacrifice – went on there, at midsummer, to make the animals breed and the corn grow. The phallic element is present in the huge erect stones. The circle itself is the black sun of winter. The offered throat of a bullock, a chant, a stone knife – these instruments and elements were required before the ceremony was complete and the honey-dripping lord of summer walked in power through the sky.

*

For weeks before midsummer the young men and women of every island gathered fuel, anything at all that would burn – bundles of heather, dry cow droppings, sea-warped boards – and carried them to the summit of the highest hill. Just before the torch was brought an animal bone was carefully inserted into the heart of the pyre – a remnant of the sacrifice of an entire beast. The torch was thrust in. Fire answered fire from the hill-tops, till all Orkney was a dapple of flame and shadow in the midsummer midnight. It was the great Johnsmas Fire, that would ensure fertility to the whole community that year.

Every peasant had his private torch of dry heather. He lit it at the fire on the hilltop and brought it carefully down to his own croft. Then, slowly and solemnly, he carried the small flame round the bounds of his field, round house and byre and barn. So he claimed a share of the sun's bounty for his family and stock. The blessing had been brought to the furrows.

At the fire on the hilltop the young men and women danced among the flames till morning. They had a part in this rite of fertility also. What is the dance but a stylised masque of coupling? The fire, symbol of all their unrequited lusts, ensured that there would be a new strong generation of islanders, new furrows, new hearth stones. The fiddles ranted on. The ale-cog went from mouth to mouth. The feet rose and fell.

Down below the fields of Orkney were green with the first shoots.

In August the fields would be yellow, as if the sun had stamped its own image on the furrows. The benign fire in the sky had sealed a blessing on the labour of men and beasts.

In all these primitive ceremonies music and the dance have an important place. The trows – embodiments of the dark potent earth energies, both good and evil – loved music and dancing. Time and again in the folk tales the fiddler is dragged down under the furrows, among roots and skulls.

Nowadays our western art is autonomous, private, a cold lonely kingdom. It presents us with the human condition but makes no claim to do anything about it; being cut off from labours and hungers; being the preserve of sophisticated people, a small priesthood who can appreciate and understand, they alone.

'Art must be of *use*,' says Storm Kolson, the old blind Orkney fiddler – 'a coercive rhyme, to strand a whale on the rock, a scratch on stone to make the corn grow. What are all these statues and violins and calf-bound editions for?'

And he remembered, as an example of true art, 'a stone between field and beach. Some fisherman with a plough had scratched on it a fish and a cornstalk – wind and wave going through both in a single wavering fruitful line.'

The ancient magical ceremonial quality of art makes it profoundly suspect to all puritans, hedonists, humanists, democrats, pragmatists, rationalists, progressives; and nowadays nearly everyone fits into one or other of these categories. The medieval Church had the wisdom to make music and art handmaidens of the faith. The Calvinists looked on beauty as a lure of the devil, and but that King David had harped before the Lord and sung psalms, one guesses there would have been no singing in their kirks. They kept the visual arts severely in check; their kirks and meeting houses were plain, severe, unadorned.

But music, dancing, poetry were too deeply woven into the nature of country people to be easily eradicated. They saw the dance as the essence of all their labour; all their goings and comings with plough and sickle and quern-stone were gathered into the fiddler's reel.

Storm Kolson said to the astonished harvesters in the oatfield of Skaill: 'The dance is a rising and falling of feet like unto your labour, a good circling, and from this pure source, the Dance (that was in the beginning with God), issue all the slow laborious necessary diurnal rounds whereby men earn with pain their bread. The dance is but a quintessence of all your work. To the dance your toil returns again, as weariness goeth to the well for refreshment . . . Let not your boat be sent down the beach unless a fiddle be there to make good its going. Let not plough be put to acre except a fiddle cross first the furrow. Let not those new married seek their bed before the chamber that they purpose to lie in be purified with music . . .'

Dance was their difficult labour turned into a gay ritual. Bread and ale were the fruits of their labour. There was a connection, therefore, between music and bread; they recognised that they were in the presence of a mystery and that they themselves were a part of it. The rhythms of art were closely related to the seasonal rhythms, to a dark potent chthonic energy that raised cornstalk and rose from their roots underground. Grave and womb deepened the mystery; in those darknesses, too, new life quickened and burgeoned. Ploughing and love have always been linked in the imagination of farmers.

> As I was ploughing in my field
> The hungriest furrow ever torn
> Followed my plough and she did cry
> 'Have you seen my mate John Barleycorn?'
>
> Says I, 'Has he got a yellow beard?
> Is he always whispering night and morn?
> Does he up and dance when the wind is high?'
> Says she, 'That's my John Barleycorn.
>
> One day they took a cruel knife
> (O, I am weary and forlorn!)

They struck him at his golden prayer.
They killed my priest, John Barleycorn.

They laid him on a wooden cart,
Of all his summer glory shorn,
And threshers broke with stick and stave
The shining bones of Barleycorn.

The miller's stone went round and round.
They rolled him underneath with scorn.
The miller filled a hundred sacks
With the crushed pride of Barleycorn.

A baker came by and bought his dust.
That was a madman, I'll be sworn.
He burned my hero in a rage
Of twisting flames, John Barleycorn.

A brewer came by and stole his heart.
Alas, that ever I was born!
He thrust it in a brimming vat
And drowned my dear John Barleycorn.

And now I travel narrow roads,
My hungry feet are dark and worn,
But no one in this winter world
Has seen my dancer Barleycorn'.

I took a bannock from my bag.
Lord, how her empty mouth did yawn!
Says I, 'Your starving days are done
For here's your lost John Barleycorn.'

I took a bottle from my pouch,
I poured out whisky in a horn.
Says I, 'Put by your grief, for here
Is the merry blood of Barleycorn.'

She ate, she drank, she laughed, she danced,
And home with me she did return.
By candle light in my old straw bed
She wept no more for Barleycorn.

Death was the third part of this trinity; and all three were
gathered up into the crowning idea of resurrection. The crofter
could not fail to be impressed by this. For him life and death
were not stark opposites but woven the one into the other, a
seamless garment. He ate his bread and drank his ale in the
depths of winter. Every April ditch, though half full of snow,
teemed with re-birth. He lived in his fathers who had
ploughed the acre before him and in his sons who would
reap it after him; he was beyond the reach of destruction.

These profound frightening mysterious energies lay deep
in the earth the crofter tilled. The same energies were present
to him in a delightful way in fiddle music and ballad. He was
a part of the earth, he was a part of the dance.

So, at midsummer, the music disappears into the earth for
the tryst of light and darkness; and the artist returns again,
strong, transfigured, timeless. The mediocre musician goes
home alone.

'Darst thu gang b' the black furrow
This night, thee and thy song?' . . .
'Wet me mooth wi' the Lenten ale,
I'll go along'.

They spied him near the black furrow
B' the glim o' the wolf star.
Slow the dance was in his feet,
Dark the fiddle he bore.

There stood three men at the black furrow
And one was clad in grey.
No mortal hand had woven that claith
B' the sweet light o' day.

There stood three men at the black furrow
And one was clad in green.
They're taen the fiddler b' the hand
Where he was no more seen.

There stood three men at the black furrow
And one was clad in yellow.
They've led the fiddler through a door
Where never a bird could follow.

They've put the gowd cup in his hand,
Elfin bread on his tongue.
There he bade a hunder years,
Him and his lawless song.

'Darst thu gang through the black furrow
On a mirk night, alone?' . . .
'I'd rather sleep wi' Christen folk
Under a kirkyard stone'.

THE MIDWINTER MUSIC

IN THE northern islands December is a
dark month. The lamps are burning when people go to their
work. Light thickens again in the early afternoon. The
weather, more often than not, is cold and stormy. There are
also calm clear nights when the hemisphere of sky is hung
with stars and in the north the Aurora Borealis rustles like
curtains of heavy yellow silk.

It is the season of The Nativity. It is also the time of trows.
To the islanders the earth they tilled was an element of
dark dangerous contending energies. The good energy of
the earth raised their crops into the sun and rain and wind;
but there were other earth energies bent on famine, sickness,
death. These energies were active always; especially in the
dark cold time of the year when nothing grew, the earth
seemed to belong to them entirely. The island farmers knew
this evil brood as trows, and the trows were more than vague
abstract energies, they had shape and substance; they could
dance, they could speak, they could travel between the hill
and the ploughed field, they were often seen (but only by
people who had the gift). The trows belonged to the under-

world, to the kingdom of night. Hideous shapes, they represented all the curses of unredeemed nature. The best way to contain the kingdom of winter and death was to lead a decent life, for the trows were among other things embodiments of the seven deadly sins; and it was best to observe duly the rituals of Christianity as well as other rituals that were old when the megalithic people built the stones at Brodgar.

The corn and the animals had to be protected. The trows grew strong and bold in winter in proportion as the creatures of light paled and dwindled. Straws in the form of a cross were fixed to the lintels of barn and byre. So these places were 'sained', made holy. The most precious creatures in a croft, and the most liable to corruption, were the children. A special care was taken of them on Helya's Night, the twentieth of December. In Shetland, the old grandmother went round each bed and cradle and committed the young ones to the care of the Virgin Mary.

> Mary Midder, had[1] de haund
> Ower aboot for sleeping-baund,
> Had da lass and had da wife,
> Had da bairn a' its life.
> Mary Midder, had de haund
> Roond da infants o' oor laund.

This beautiful poem was being uttered in the north three and a half centuries after the Reformation.

If the children were not protected it was easy for the trows to steal them. What happened was this: the trows left their own offspring in the cradle, and these winter children generally grew up sick and deformed. So the people say of someone who looks permanently ill that he is 'trowie'.

A great peace and silence fell on the islands on Thomasmas, the twenty-first of December, and continued till after Christmas. No work was done, except what was absolutely essential.

[1] Hold, keep.

> The very babe unborn
> Cries O dul![1] dul!
> For the breaking o'
> > Thammasmas Night
> Five nights afore Yule.

They called December the twenty-third Modra Night. It was the longest night of the year and so the mother of all other nights. And possibly it was the night when the Mother of God, heavy with her burden, set out on the road to Bethlehem.

December the twenty-fourth was a night specially holy and terrible. The trows, in dark hordes, lingered outside every croft. The crofter removed the upper quernstone from the lower. All through the year the women had ground the corn, turning the quernstones in fruitful sunwise circles. It was certain that the trows, given the chance, would secretly turn the quern widdershins, against the sun, so that the stones would be rendered barren and the family would starve during the following year.

The terror of darkness was held in check by a strictly-observed ritual. The mother brought out a basin and filled it with water. The man of the house, priest-like, took three live embers from the fire and dropped them in the water. So, in midwinter, the elements of fire and water were true to the tryst of purification. They would meet and mell in their other dance, fecundity, in spring-time. Let the shrunken earth abide the lustful embraces of sun and rain in the time of seed; tonight all three met in a trance of purity.

In this condensed drama all nature – light and darkness, the four elements, plant and beast and man – were seen as part of a divine festival. The creatures of nature kept their trysts in season, they could not behave otherwise. Man, with his scattered and distracted energies, the flesh tugging forever

[1] Woe.

against the spirit, 'born under one law, to another bound,' moving between the trow-infested earth and the angel-fretted sky, proclaimed his allegiance to the kingdom of light (of which he was the shining wayward heir) in the form of a willed and strictly-observed ritual; as now, when the priest-like crofter, his dwindled fields all around him, mingled the elements of fire and water; for a purification, that his winter-beleaguered household might be worthy to eat bread, a mingling of his own harrow-sweat with heaven's grace . . . One by one, each member of the family washed himself all over in the fire-kissed water and put on clean clothes. The rooms had been swept already; everything dirty had been bundled away; the dishes on the dresser glinted in the lamp-light. The children were put to bed. Midnight was approaching. The other members of the family retired one by one, until only the parents were left. They made then an act of great faith. Though the night outside was thick with trows, they unfastened the door and left the lamp burning and went to bed. It was possible that Our Lady and Saint Joseph with their as-yet-hidden treasure would come to their croft that night, seeking shelter.

Early on Christmas morning the man of the house rose before daybreak, while the others were still asleep. He lit a candle in the skull of a cow, carefully fixing it in the eye-socket. He went into the byre, carrying this lantern. He fed the beasts by its light, giving them more to eat than usual. It was a re-enaction of the scene in the byre at Bethlehem; the animals had also been present at Christ's nativity. The flame in the skull was a reminder to them that they shared both in mortality and in this blessed time, the kindling of the one true light in the world's darkness.

There was nothing to be afraid of now. The trows had returned to their burrows, defeated. Christ was born among the fields.

The children were awake when the crofter came back. They

had a small candle each that they lit and set here and there about the room. The crofter filled a bowl with whisky – quintessence of earth's ripeness, the heavy rich blood of summer; solemnly he carried the bowl to each person in turn; even the children had to wet their lips. The bread lay on the table – not the coarse everyday bannock, but Yule-brunnies, little round yellow cakes of rye and fat, pinched at the edges to represent the sun's rays; a Yule-brunnie for everyone in the house. The Christmas breakfast was a festival of candle light. The eating of the cakes was a kind of pre-Christian non-sacramental communion. In the heart of winter they devoured the sun, and so filled their days with light and gaiety and fruitfulness.

A few fields away from the Ring of Brodgar in Stenness is the grass-covered hemisphere of Maeshowe. There is no doubt about Maeshowe; it is a burial chamber, a kingdom of the dead, where the 'silent vanished races' laid chiefs and high-born maidens in a mathematical-astronomical stone web, a dome of immense quarried monoliths. A long low passage leads from the light into this petrified womb, which remains in perpetual darkness except (it is said) for one brief moment every year. On midwinter day, just before the ultimate darkness – 'the year's midnight' – the setting sun shines through the long passage and throws one fleeting golden look on the opposite wall. It is a pledge that, after the long night of winter and death, the earth, with all its freight of seed and root and jewelled bones, will proceed to resurrection and the spring-time.

Yule is the festival of innocence. New Year, seven days later, is the festival of experience, that measures time and hopes and dreads everything.

The young men gather, a group of a dozen or more singers, on the last night of the year. Among them is the Fool, whom they call the 'kairyin horse', the beast of burden, the scapegoat. A curse and a blessing are on him; he is liable to be roughly handled by the choir of young men, kicked and thrown about, whenever the fancy takes them; but when it comes to the distribution of food and drink he is given a larger share than the others, and this too as the old year dies becomes a further occasion for recrimination and insult.

The family round the peat fire hear a distant singing on the road, in the darkness of the last night of the year.

> Guid be tae this buirdly bigging!
> > *We're a' Saint Mary's men*
> Fae the steethe-stane tae the rigging
> > *Fore wur Lady*
>
> Guid bless the guidwife an' sae the guidman
> > *We're a' Saint Mary's men*
> Dish an' table, pot an' pan
> > *Fore wur Lady*

The crofter takes the door off the latch. The croft lamp throws a weak waver of light outside. The singers stand at the edge of it, a glitter of eyes. They chant.

> This night is guid New'ar ev'n's night
> > *We're a' Saint Mary's men*
> An' we've come here tae crave wur right
> > *Fore wur Lady*
>
> The morn it is guid New'ar Day
> > *We're a' Saint Mary's men*
> An' we've come here tae sport and play
> > *Fore wur Lady*

Neighbours are calling with good wishes to neighbour. Yet the refrain insists that the neighbourliness is not entirely secular. The Virgin Mary, Our Lady, Queen of Heaven, is also invited to be present. (We can assume the sacred chorus for the rest of the song.) Secular and holy link hands in the dance.

A light threatening tone enters; but however the mood changes – and the song is full of twists and turns – the festive note is constant.

> An' if we get no' what we seek
> We'll tak the head of your Yule sheep.

The blessing is resumed, is broadened to include all the creatures of stable and byre and barnyard. The crofter opens the door a little further. A cow lows in the byre, pigs shift and grunt in the stye. The women and children listen beside the fire. A kirn of ale seethes in a dark corner. The table is loaded with cheese, boiled fowls, bannocks, slices of mutton. The song runs on through the sluice of the open door, merry as a winter burn in spate.

> May a' your kye be weel tae calf
> An' every ane hae a queyo calf
>
> May a' your mares be weel tae foal
> An' every ane hae a mare foal
>
> May a' your yowes[1] be weel tae lamb
> An' every ane hae a yowe an' a ram
>
> May a' your geese be weel tae t'rive
> An' every ane hae three times five
>
> May a' your hens rin in a reel
> An' every ane twal' at her heel.

Now the song leaves the bare winter farmstead and enters a vernal world, a region of romance. King Henry of England and his mistress are in the greenwood. Sailors, friars, wander-

[1] Ewes.

ing masons have brought stories of English chivalry into the north; but what have these splendid figures to do with the island crofter and his wife, worn to the bone with year-long labour? It is, among other things, an insistence on the dignity and beauty of every life, however humble. In the eye of Our Lady of Heaven, who presides over the song, the good man and the good-wife are as worthy as King Henry and Rosamund – more worthy, for their life is not a passing vernal lust, it is rooted in the real world, pasture and dung and tilth. The crofter is lord in a more lasting kingdom, where poverty and riches have other meanings; he and his people are heirs of a heavenly hoard. Only seven nights back didn't Our Lady give birth to the King of kings in a byre? As this little inset lyric glows and throbs, it is hard to tell what Lady is being praised – Rosamund or Mary crowned with stars – so mixed are secular and divine in the song.

> King Henry he is no' at hame
> But he is tae the greenwids gane
>
> Wi' him are baith his hawk an' hound
> An' the fair Lady Rosamund
>
> We'll tell you hoo wur queen is drest
> If you will gae us o' your best
>
> She wears upon her head aye
> The golden croon sae red aye
>
> She wears upon her breest bane
> The glitterin' brooches many a ane
>
> She wears upon her middle sma'
> The gilt an' golden girdle a'
>
> She wears upon her legs' sheen
> Stockings o' the red tameen

> She wears upon her feet aye
> The cordiner shoon sae neat aye.

Has the lovely lyric not melted their hearts? Why have the singers not been ushered inside, as in former years? Surely something evil and sinister has happened! Perhaps they are singing to four doomed tenantless walls. Kirn and pot will be for ever empty; the hearth unswept, the planticru undug. . . . The voices in the night are heavy with foreboding; the rhymes are uncertain; the song is like to gutter entirely. This part of the song is an utterance of warning concerning the poverty into which a crofter's estate can sink if he leaves the smallest chink for weed and rat to enter; or perhaps only if he shuts himself from the blessing of the New Year Song, which is both earthly and heavenly.

At this point the man of the house open his door wide, so that he stands framed in the lamplight, and the singers can see the compact excited family round the fire; and the grandmother and the children can see the circle of ghosts with red merry mouths in the frosty darkness outside.

> Whaur is the guidman o' this hoose?
> Whaur is he, that man?
>
> An' why is he no' as before
> At the opening o' the door?
>
> Whaur is the guidwife o' this hoose?
> Whaur is she, that dame?
>
> An' why is she no' as before
> Wi' her full cog under faim?[1]
>
> Whaur is the servant lass o' this hoose?
> Whaur is she, that lass?

[1] Ale keg with a head of froth on it.

143

And why is she no' as afore
In sweepin' oot the asse?

Whaur is the servant man o' this hoose?
Whaur is he, that lad?

And why is he no as afore
Oot dellin' wi' a spade?

This night is guid New'ar ev'n's night
An' we've come here tae claim wur right.

Now the singers have a full view of the loaded table inside.
All is well with this farm after all, thank God. Let the crofter
and his wife do their duty then. The choir is cold and hungry.
If these bearers of luck and blessing receive their due, good
fortune will bide in this house in the year to come. The wheel
turns; the *de profundis* chant becomes suddenly a fantasy of
wealth and abundance. They will be richer than the laird
himself. They will have wide acres and trading ships on the
sea. The flattery merges into a ritual boasting that includes the
whole community of the island in wished-for prosperity and
affluence – all except the mean wife where they last visited;
what the singers will do to her they hint at darkly and lewdly.

Guidman, go tae your geelin-vat[1]
An' fetch us here a quart o' that

Fetch us ane, and fetch us twa
An' we'll gang the merrier awa'

Guidwife, go to your butter ark
An' weigh us oot o' that ten mark

Guidman, go to your bacon
And cut us doon a daggon[2]

[1] Vessel for making ale.   [2] Chunk.

144

Cut it lucky, cut it room,
Look 'at you dunno cut your toom[1]

Guidwife, go to your cubby creel
An' what you cut, try cut it weel

The last hoose that we were at
'Twas there we got but ae bere cake[2]

The jade that baked it sae thin
Merry an' wanton may she rin

We will ca' snitter in her tow[3]
An burn it in a red red lowe

An' when that red lowe is gane
She will get a waurlike shame

We hae wur ships sailan the sea
An mighty men o lands are we

We hae war stacks stanein'
And we hae wur ploos gangin'

We hae wur fat gilts in the stye,
A few tae sell and nane tae buy.

Yes, all this wealth would be theirs in actual fact, but for one dreadful burden that they must bear all the days of their life; and with one accord they turn on the clown of the party, the 'kairyin horse', whose duty it is to hump round the surplus food and drink that has been given them in the various crofts, and they kick him and buffet him in mock earnest; for the singers and the crofter their host would indeed be rich farmers and traders were they not kept in poverty by the inordinate appetites of their beast to whom they have been so good. The Fool symbolises now prodigality, wastefulness, gluttony, stupidity, all that drags a man and his estate into

---

[1] Thumb.   [2] Barley scone.   [3] Pull her hair.

penury, all the taxes and stipends and feus and excise duties and rents that keep him bound for ever to the plough and the grindstone.

> Here we hae wur kairyin horse
> An' muckle vengence fa' his corse
>
> For he wad eat mair meat
> Or a' that we can gaither an get
>
> An' he wad drink mair drink
> Or a' that we can swither or swink

With a wild mixture of threatening, cajolery, joy, impudence the song ends. The door is flung wide. Faces pinched with the cold crowd about the blazing peat-fire and festive board. The meal is eaten standing. It is a reward for all the labour of the past year that has been done in the parish, a gathering of strength for the work of the year to come, a ritual feast rounded with song and dancing and prayer.

> Be ye maids or be ye nane
> Ye's a' be kissed or we gang hame
>
> Wur shoon they're made o' mare's hide
> Wur feet's sae cauld we canna bide
>
> An if you dunno open your door
> We'll lay it flat upon the floor
>
> Guidwife, just lift your ambry lid
> An' fetch the busslins an' the redd[1]
>
> An' the three-lugged cog that's standing fu'
> Fetch it here tae weet wur mou'
>
> This is the best that we can tak'
> An' we will drink till wur lugs crack

---

[1] Puddings and haggis.

This is the sevent' night o Yule
We're a' Saint Mary's men
An' b' me saul, I think it'll fail
Fore wur Lady

5

POETS

THE BALLAD SINGER

ROBERT RENDALL

THE BALLAD SINGER

THE FIRE leapt high in the immense hearth. The ladies sat as near the candles as they could; their needles drew long coloured threads through the linen. Servant girls hurried to carry platters, and empty flagons, and gnawed bones, down to the kitchen. The ballad singer, dappled with flame, stood near the hearth; he could not begin until the great ones had taken their places. The earl and his factor and the sheriff and the two Cathedral canons were still arguing over the dregs of the claret: thus the array should have been drawn up, thus the cavalry disposed with the shoulder of the hill cutting off the arrows' trajectory, and so Flodden would have been a Scottish field. ... But no, said Master Lorimer the sheriff (who drank no claret but lipped a glass of water from time to time), happening thus as it happened, it was God's will 'ab origine', and King James was a dead man before ever he spurred his horse out of the courtyard of Holy Rood.

No one spoke to the ballad singer. The tapestry undulated along one wall; the chamber was full of little winds that fluttered the candles and made Alysoun wish she had brought her woollen wrap to cover her bare arms. A red-faced country girl carried the last clattering plates out into the corridor, directed by Mistress Coubister the housekeeper who stood beside the curtain with her best lace shawl about her. The earl wiped his lips with linen – thick red moist Stuart mouth – and rose to his feet. Canon by canon rose. The factor rose. The sheriff rose. The ladies rose. The earl moved to his oak chair beside the fire. The hound flowed after him and lay down at his feet with sad abject eyes, fallen dewlaps, lolling tongue. The canons and the factor and the sheriff sat down again. The ladies, gently, with a clean swish of linen, sat down. Canon Fulzie filled his pewter with claret, a red minuscule music. The earl inclined his head; now he was ready. The ballad singer stepped forward. The ladies inclined their heads. Cold Alysoun left her needle dangling from the half-finished fleur-de-lys on her linen and inclined her head and listened. All listened.

> In Norowa a lady bade,
>   A bonny lass in muckle gear,
> And it was soothly sung and said,
>   She was a lady sweet and fair.
>
> Them cam' fae east and west i' pride
>   An' some cam sailan owre the sea,
> An' a' tae win her for a bride;
>   But never a bride wad the lady be.
>
> She bade them gang heem[1] an' mend their claes[2]
>   That they had worn in comin' sae far,
> She ca'd them fules, she ca'd them flaes,
>   Set stooks on them and gae them a skar.[3]
>
> There was a man baith stoor and strang
>   An' he wis neeméd Odivere;
> He lo'ed the sword, he lo'ed the sang,
>   But aye he lo'ed the lasses mair.

[1] Go home.   [2] Clothes.   [3] Frightened them.

This Odivere fell on his knee
    An vooed a voo upo' his life,
And swore b' him that hang on tree[1]
    To mak' this lady fair his wife.

He's coorted her, he's wedded her,
    An' they were blithe and blissfu' baith;
An' aye he bragged near and far
    He won his wife b' Odin's oath.

He's left her in his boorly ha',
    A-greetan sair that dolefu' day;
Tae Guthaland[2] he's gaen awa'
    The muckle pagan loons to slay.

As he cam' back fae Guthaland
    I' Muckle Gerth[3] be bade awhile,
An' foys and fiechtins had tae hand
    For ladies fair did him beguile.

At Muckle Gerth he tarried lang –
    Black sight[4] on him for bidan there!
While sat i' dule her maids amang
    Wi' tearful e'e his lady fair.

An' aft she boonied hersel sae braw,
    An' aft her gowden hair wad keem,
An' then look owre the castle wa
    To see her ain good-man come heem.

An' aye she looked an' lippened[5] lang
    For many a dowie day an' year;
But Odivere, he didna come,
    Nor word o' Oddie could she hear.

The poet paused. He looked speculatively over the intent
heads. He himself was a person of no consequence; at the end

[1] Not Christ, but Odin.   [2] The Holy Land (literally, God's Land).
[3] Byzantium.   [4] The evil eye.   [5] Expected.

of the entertainment he would be given a groat, or a crown (depending on the earl's whim), and a supper of porridge and ale, and a bed between the sergeant of guard's bed and the palace carpenter's bed. He was nothing; but while the ballad lasted these great ones of Orkney were his utterly, he could make them laugh or weep as he chose, or beg for more like dogs. His slow formal chant probed them to their innermost sanctuaries; showed them, beneath their withering faces, the enduring skull; but hinted also at an immortal pearl lost under the vanities and prodigalities of their days. Already little Alysoun, the earl's latest mistress, looked about her with a white pinched face. How strange it was (thought Alysoun), the tide of lust and liking, with its ebb and flow like the sea! A girl that had been cold and still as a pool all her life – one day a glance or a word made her lance and burn like fire. Alysoun knew exactly how it was with the Lady Odivere. Last April she herself had been a Birsay lass among the other Birsay lasses, keeping the cows out of the ploughed rig, winding straw ropes in the barn, running across the meadow with the new grass under their bare feet, a chorus of shrill wind-disordered laughter. . . . Then one morning at the beach Jacob the fisherman had spoken to the paddling girls, telling them not to dance in the pool above their thighs or they would be cold maidens till white hairs and death; and at that moment Alysoun's heart faltered and failed inside her with desire. . . . But what was the good of it, Jacob hardly looked at her, he had his woman Katrin that he visited nightly at Greenay hill, to him Alysoun was only a silly farm-lass. Yet for a long month Alysoun was up every dawn to help Jacob launch his lobster boat, and she was at the beach, faithful as sunset, when he rowed in from the west. And Jacob would speak to her kindly, and give her a crab out of his catch, never seeming to realise the flames and frosts that were eroding Alysoun's heart. . . . Alysoun had prayed in the kirk to Our Lady and Saint Magnus – even though this past winter or two such idolatry had been strictly forbidden – to make Jacob look kindly on her, so kindly that he would forget Katrin and think only of Alysoun as his woman. And to reinforce her petition she had done what every country lass did, gone out to the standing stone under the new moon and said the love charm that Jeannag the hen wife had taught her – no Odin oath, but a rigmarole that she could by no means make sense of. And the spell had worked, though perversely; because suddenly peedie Alysoun became a desirable woman. One evening two horsemen from the palace summoned her, as she was clambering down from the links to the shore to help Jacob haul his boat up; and before midnight, bathed and perfumed and satined, she was drinking wine in the earl's bed-chamber, the most favoured and fortunate lass in Orkney, with a single red candle burning at the wall. . . . Yet that night and every night for a month it was still Jacob Mowat the fisherman she thought of in the darkness, stripped of her satin, and it was Jacob's fish-scale arms that girded her, and Jacob's sweet lewd mouth that suggested this and that into her glutted ear.

Now, three months later – so moon-drawn are the tides of lust and liking – she never thought about the fisherman and his Katrin at all. To Jeannag the hen-wife she had sent at Johnsmas a little leather bag with seven silver French crowns in it. Her father's farm was richer by two garron mares and a Highland bull and a stye-full of pigs and twelve acres, his neighbours Walter Neilson and Thomas Wylie having been summarily evicted to make way for the earl's honorary good-father.

Yet this was certain (as already was foreshadowed in the ballad), in the end all species of enchantment brought nothing but heartbreak and loss. Alysoun knew that her brief summer was nearly over. What would happen to her, when the earl began to give her cold looks? She knew this, two nights in the past week – the time she had been indisposed with her lunar bleedings – Earl Patrick had been closeted with Sigrid Sinclair, a lass from Westray who made cheese and butter in the palace kitchen; and what was Andrew Keir, the Kirkwall timber and spirit importer, lying in the dungeon for this past fortnight but that the earl might have free access to Andrew Keir's young comely unfruited wife? The whole palace knew about that, and some looked with pity at Alysoun and others smirked as she passed them on the long twisting stair.

Alysoun's own reflection looked fearfully back at her from the tender pitiful ballad of the Lady Odivere. So cruel are the tides of lust and liking! Alysoun rose up and glided over the whispering rushes on the floor and sat down at the earl's feet and put her small bright head on his knee. The dog regarded her sadly.

The ballad singer began again.

> At e'enin i' the mirkin[1] o't
>   A stately knight cam' tae her ha'.
> Fu' lood he chappéd on the yett
>   And loodly at the yett did ca'.
>
> 'A boon, a boon! ye porter loon,
>   Bed me this nicht within your ha'.
> Me vista's lang, the nicht is mirk,
>   An' home and haudin far awa'.'
>
> 'Begone, begone, awa, awa!
>   To bed you here that may not be.
> Nae stranger sleeps within this ha'
>   While my good lord's ayont the sea.'
>
> 'Gin you wad no' find the weight o' me hand,
>   Gae tell your lady mistress fair
> That I hae come fae Guthaland
>   An' bear her word o' Odivere.'

[1] Darkening.

The yett was opened at his word,
  An' boldly strode he in the ha'.
And a' the women roond him said
  A stoorer knight they never saw.

An' he's taen off his silken cap
  An' he's gaen doon apo his knee
And he's laid a gowd ring on the lady's lap
  That she was unco fain to see.

'A token fae thee husband dear
  I bring tae thee, my lady fair,
I left him weel, i' jolly cheer.
  They ca' him noo, Sir Odivere.

'An' weel he's won his knight's degree.
  B' slaying many a soldier stoor,
An' makan hosts o' pagans flee
  Afore his sword sae sharp an' door.'

When she the gowden ring had seen
  She took nae tent o' what he said
But drew her kerchief owre her een,
  An' colour fae her fair face fled.

But syne her bonny face grew bright
  An' blithely blinked her bonny e'e.
'Rise up, rise up, ye valiant knight
  For oncons[1] guid ye bring to me.

'A stately bulie[2] i' the ha',
  Pour oot the best o' blude-red wine,
Wi' futh[3] o' a' that's guid and braw
  That this brave knight fu' weel may dine.'

An' many a tale he told that nicht
  O' tulyies[4] focht for ladies fair

[1] News, tidings.   [2] Feast.   [3] Abundance.   [4] Contests.

An' a' aboot that worthy knight
   I' Guthaland, Sir Odivere.

He minted[1] aye, tho, he never said,
   An' skeeted[2] aye i' ilka tale,
That Odivere was a rovin' blade
   An' liked the lasses ower weel.

An' when the bulie was fairly done
   An' a' the servants gaen tae bed
An' the twa themsels were left alane
   The lady to the stranger said:

'Why bring ye back that gowden ring
   That brings to me sair dule and pain,
That minds me o' the blithesome days
   When I o' thee was ower fain?'

'Ye ken, fair dame, to me aye dear,
   Lang syne ye gae that ring to me,
An' on this ring i' the moon-licht clear
   Ye swore for ever mine to be.

'An' I i' dule hae gaen sin' syne,
   A lanely man on land an' sea,
An' never a face hae seen but thine
   That I could spier me wife to be'.

'Noo wheesht, noo wheest, ye fause-tongued knight,
   Your words will work me muckle skaith.
Full weel ken ye what sundered us
   — It was the dowie Odin's aith.'

He's taen her white hand i' his stately nave,[3]
   An' fain was she, an' fain was he.
What happened next, ye need no' speer;[4]
   In sooth I wisna dare to see.

---

[1] Hinted.   [2] Insinuated.   [3] Fist.   [4] Inquire.

> The knight's awa' i' morning grey,
>   He bade no' for a farewell foy.
> What naebody kens naebody can say;
>   But the lady's left i' peerie[1] joy.
>
> Her bony e'en blinked no sae bright,
>   Her red and white grew white an' grey,
> An' ilka day she wished for nicht
>   An' ilka nicht she wished for day.

The voice darkened and dropped, but the pulse throbbed on and on through twenty stretched minds, through the single cunningly-tuned harp of their imagination.

It is well enough, Earl Patrick Stuart thought, to read a poem out of a manuscript, privately, or to finger a flute in the loneliness of your bedchamber, well and pleasant it is, but there is nothing like an interlude where a group of people take part, both as players and audience, a concert, a communion in which the bread of art is broken and shared; this is entirely delightful.

The earl loved beauty in all its forms – a house built with blocks of red and grey stone, turrets, an Italian garden at one side; or a pavane on a summer evening with viol and lute playing one against the other, a sweet counterpoint; or the young men of Holy Rood, exquisite as peacocks, speaking epigrams in French and Italian, showing off their flowered waistcoats and their codpieces. If only government was an art also, and could compel people as surely as this rhymster! God had not willed it so. Men were a perverse clay to mould – flatterers, fawners, fleeting as butterflies, thick as oxen. Let you but try to govern a people never so well – observing always the God-ordained order of society, first the king, then earl and bishop, then the gentry and the lesser clergy, then merchants and farmers, then the anonymous horde of peasants and fishermen and tradesmen, with its fringe of mendicants and

[1] Small.

tinkers and gangrels, so that all got their due – let you but try to make music upon that instrument, no sound came from it but a hellish screeching and yowling. . . . God had fashioned him, like all his royal race, to be an artist, not to order the affairs of some barbarous ungrateful Norwegian islanders. But for a day such as this, once or twice in the week – coursing of hares in the morning along the Birsay links, roast pig and claret and talk with Canon Fulzie in the late afternoon, dancing and poetry in the evening, then the darkness with Alysoun his dove – but for these interludes the duties that had been put on him were indeed a bitter draught to stomach. Poetry above all was his consolation; there all he wrestled with in the council chamber every morning, brutality, perversity, stupidity, ugliness, was gathered into the cold perfection of language. He could look on life as it was viewed, perhaps, by an angel's eye, *sub specie aeternitatis*.

Some man, a familiar stranger, had wormed his way into the hall of the Lady Odivere and showed her a ring as a token of former understanding between them; yes, and more than that, he had wormed his way into her bed and her body; and in the morning had ridden off again.

Her red and white grew white and grey.

He lipped the words silently, relishing them like small sips of wine.

How else to describe the wilting of a lass betrayed?

When that old woman, Sophia Gunn in Watten, Caithness, had written to him last winter that her daughter Madge that had been a seamstress two months in the palace was with child to him, and poured out a long list of symptoms, together with girnings and imprecations, page after page till he was like a spew with scunner, how much better if she had written simply, 'Her red and white grows white and grey.' . . . Then truly he might have given the old hag and the young hag a

pension to have seen them through till some red-faced farmer
was found to marry Madge and foster her bairn.

But now the poet was clearing his throat again.

I heard a lady ba'an her bairn,
   An' aye she rockit, an' aye she sang,
An' took sae hard apo the verse
   Till the he'rt within her body rang.

'Ba loo, ba, loo, me bonny bairn,
   Ba loo lillie, ba loo lay,
Sleep thu, me peerie bonie budo!
   Thu little kens thee mither's wae.

'Aloor! I dinna ken thee faither.
   Aloor, aloor! me waeful sin!
I dinna ken me bairn's faither
   Nor yet the land that he lives in.

'Aloor, aloor! ca'd sall I be
   A wicked woman b' a' men,
That I, a married wife, soud hae
   A bairn tae him I dunno ken.'

Then up an' spak a grimly gest[1]
   That stood sae lech at her bed feet,
'O here I am, thee bairn's faither,
   Although I'm no' thee husband sweet.'

'Me bairn's faither I ken thu are,
   Nae luve sae sweet I'll ever hae,
An' yet I hae a guid, guid man
   That's far awa' fae me this day.'

'I care no' for thee wedded carl,
   I wish his face I'll never see,

[1] Apparition.

But when six months is come an' gane
   I'll come an' play the noris fee.[1]

'It's no be said thu tint[2] b' me
   A bodle worth o' worldly gare,
So when I come, thu'll get thee fee
   An' I me bairn to be me heir.'

'Noo, for the love I bore tae thee,
   A love that's brought me muckle shame,
O tell me where thee home may be,
   An' tell me true thee vera name?'

'San Imravoe it is me name,
   I gang on land and swim on sea,
Among the ranks o' selkie[3] folk
   I am a yarl o' high degree.

'I am a man apo the land,
   I am a selkie i' the sea,
My home it is the Soola-Skerry
   An' a' that's there is under me.

'Mair or a thoosand selkie folk
   Tae me a willing service gae,
An' I am king o' a' the folk
   An' law to them is what I say.'

'O hoo can thu thee bairn tak',
   An' hoo can thu thee bairn save?
I' thee caald home thu'll only mak
   The grimly sea me bairn's grave.'

'Me peerie bairn I'll safely ferry,
   Tho' I hae neither ship nor skift,
Wi' muckle care tae Soolis-Skerry
   Afore the sun's hich i' the lift.'

[1] Nursing fee.   [2] Lost.   [3] Seal.

'But hoo sall I me young son ken,
   An' hoo sall I me bairn know?'
'O' a' the selkies i' Soolis-Skerry
   He'll be the middlemaist o' them a'.

'His megs[1] sall a' be black as soot,
   His croopan[2] white as driven snaw,
An' I beside him, like the sam'
   I was tae thee i' times awa'.'

'Me ain guidman's a warrior prood
   An' aye a stival nave[3] has he,
An' he may prick or club me bairn
   When he's a selkie i' the sea.'

'I fear no that, I fear but this
   That cockcraa comes an' finds me here,
But come what may, I come again
   An' fetch me bairn in ae half-year.

'For then will be a seventh stream,
   An' then again a man I'll be,
An' tak' me bonny peerie bairn
   A' tae the boons o' Soolis-Skerry.'

When the six months were come and gane
   He cam' to pay the noris fee.
The tane o' his hands was fu' o' gowd,
   The tither fu' o' white monie.

The lady's taen a gowden chain,
   Her waddin' boon fae Odivere,
She tied it roond her bairn's haas,[4]
   It for her sake she bade him wear.

'I'm come to fetch me bairn awa'.
   Farewell, for thu're anither's wife.'

[1] Flippers.   [2] Body.   [3] Strong fist.   [4] Neck.

'I'll wad thee wi' a gowden ring
  An' bide beside thee a' me life.'

'Thu wadna when I wad, goodwife,
  I winno when thu're willan noo.
That day thu tint thu'll never find.
  It's late, it's owre late tae rue'.

The lady lives a lanely life,
  An' aften looks apo the sea,
Still lipenan[1] her first luve ta fin',
  But jubish[2] that can never be.

Canon Fulzie, alone at the table beyond the wavering circles of light from hearth and candles, poured a little more claret into his pewter. The fellow recited well – he did not deny it. To the canon's certain knowledge this ballad-monger was a feckless fellow, never far from ale barrels, a trouble to fisher-girls and milk-girls, a scrounger, a most rare attender at the church on Sunday; yes, and he delighted to mimic his betters, provost and factor and priest, turning their phrases and accents to exquisite mockery, and even twisting his features into passable masks of those worthy and venerable citizens, until the ploughmen laid down their ale-mugs in the tavern and bent double with loud explosions of delight.

Canon Fulzie would not give such a fellow house-room or hearing, both for that reason and for another of graver import – that the kind of poetry he represented (if you could call it poetry) was altogether perverse and dangerous, a hectic in society, a subtle searching poison.

The coupling of men and beasts! It was not only impossible foolishness, it was clean contrary to God's order of creation: namely, light and darkness, land and sea and firmament, plants, fish and animals – at last on the sixth day the supreme consummation, Man. God looked and saw that it was good.

[1] Expecting.   [2] Doubtful.

But in this kind of poetry all became chaos again, the barriers were broken down, animals usurped the sacred tongue of men and brought their seasonal lusts to the fire of love that belonged solely to the children of Adam. (It was true that in the divine poetry of Ovid, and in the prose of Lucius Apuleius, such things happened also, but these, though great artists, were pagans, and had pagans' licence to write whatsoever they chose; besides which their exquisite jewelled artistry was not to be compared to the vulgar balladry of this clown.)

What Canon Fulzie saw, and dreaded, was that the shapeless chaos of this poetry represented the total breaking up of society – was a whisper, a portent, of universal disintegration. God knows (thought the canon, his cheek almost as dark as the claret he was lipping), a flood as huge as Noah's had almost gone over Christendom a half-century ago, when the estates of Scotland decreed reformation in the kirk, and but that the clergy of Orkney had trimmed their sails and lain before the wind, the church had gone down utterly. Thanks be to God, by entering upon acceptable accommodation with nobles and commons, the kirk was still afloat (though with grievous loss of sacramental cargo). Their cathedral of Saint Magnus had not been torn down, nor made a stable for horses, nor a dance hall, and bishop and chapter still ruled in the diocese. But the position remained precarious. Master Knox and Master Melville had raged in the bare kirks of Scotland that not only Pope and Mass and statues and candles and missals and celibacy and incense must go, but bishop and prebend must follow them into the devil's darkness.

Canon Fulzie could not say what the end would be. Worse evil might come. He knew this, there was a hollowness at the centre of his life these ten years past, a hunger that none of their vaunted new liberties could satisfy. Every morning since his ordination he had woken to the delight of saying his Mass in a side chapel of the Cathedral, his soul longed for it as the hart pants for the water springs. Still every morning, though now he was an old man, he woke with the same delight; until he felt the bulk of Mistress Anne Fulzie in the bed beside him; and then began another day of doubt and questioning, and a sick waiting for news out of Scotland.

Much that was good and gracious and hallowed was breaking up, falling apart. Nothing was secure – certainly not the government in these islands of that thick-necked bastard grandson of King James the Fifth, sitting in his chair beside the fire with his hound and his whore at his feet, his full lips parted slightly with relish and anticipation. Homer and Virgil and Horace, Master Robert Henryson and Master Gavin Douglas, had gone down too before this barbarous rhymer and his quatrains; he was already speaking the first words of the fourth movement of the ballad.

Canon Fulzie consoled himself with another dollop of claret into his cup.

> So Odivere's come home again
>   Wi' muckle store o' wardly gear,
> An' he, his lady, an' his men
>   Mak' holidays wi' bulies rare.
>
> They danced and sang, they told their tales,
>   An' syne sat down tae drink and dine
> Wi' joles of flesh and fuman cogs[1]
>   An' wallie horns o bluid-red wine.
>
> Ae day says Oddie tae his men
>   'I doot gin here we langer link
> We'll a' grow fat as butterba's
>   An dee wi' futh[2] of meat an' drink.
>
> 'It's weel enough a peerie while,
>   I canna thole it lang ava.
> Let's hunt the otters on the shore
>   An' start the morn at blink o' da'.'

[1] Ale-kegs.   [2] Excess.

They hunted otters on the shore,
　　A selkie ran oot o' a geo,[1]
An' Odivere he took no lang
　　To fell him wi' a mester blow.

Then oot and spak een o' his men
　　'Far hae I sailed and muckle seen,
But never gowd on selkie's haas,
　　Till noo I see 't wi' baith me e'en.'

They bore the selkie tae the ha'
　　An' never a word said Odivere.
His face was black an' lowed his e'en
　　Though he did neither ban nor swear.

'Co' doon, co' doon! Lady Odivere,
　　Co' doon and see me ferly[2] fang.
Ye's read tae me this riddle-rae
　　B' a' the saints that ever sang!'

The lady she cam' doon tae see,
　　They made sae muckle steer.
'Here's the gowd chain ye got fae me.
　　Tell me, goodwife, hoo cam it here?'

'Aloor, aloor! me bonny bairn.
　　Me bairn! What am I born tae see?
Me malison lie on the hand
　　That's wrought this deed o' blude on thee!'

The lady wi' her torn hair
　　She was a doleful sicht tae see,
Her greetan[3] lood and sabban sair,
　　Her arms aroond the dead selkie.

'Yer bairn, guidwife! no bairn o' mine,
　　An' yet ye were me wedded wife.

---

[1] A large crag fissure.　　[2] Strange capture.　　[3] Weeping.

I doot, when I've been far fae home,
  Ye've led a wicked woman's life.'

'An' gin I be thee wedded wife,
  A wedded man wur thu tae me?
Ye left me tae a lanely life
  An' bade lang years ayont the sea.'

'I left thee wi' baith lands and gare,
  An' made thee mistress o' them a',
An' thocht thu wad be true to me
  As I to thee when far awa'.'

'Black sight apo thee lands and gare!
  Thu little kens a woman's he'rt,
To think thee gift o' worldly gare
  Is a' the lovin' husband's pert.'

'When doughty deeds were to be done
  It wad hae been a bonny pass
Had I ly'n hame tae culye[1] thee
  An' bore me fingers i' the asse.

'I couldna thole a sluggard life,
  An', lady, I wad hae thee ken
When I took thee to be me wife
  I did no' want a cluckan hen.'

'Gin I can cluck, saul thu can craw
  Owre a' thee deeds wi' women done,
Hoo ilka bonny wench thu saw
  Thu coorted her and ca'd it fun.

'But ae deid bairn, aloor, hae I!
  An' if this deed was wrang i' me,
Hoo many bairns hes thu tae shaw
  Hoo true a man thu's been tae me?

[1] Fondle.

168

'Could I no' tak what cam tae me
    Tae tempt me i' me langsome life
While thu were skalan[1] frank and free
    Thee dearest tocher o' a wife?'

'Ye lee, ye lee, lee leean limmer!
    Whare'er we drank, abune them a'
Thee weel-faur'd face I toasted aye,
    An' focht wi' him what said me na.

'An' when i' battle's saviest[2] pall,
    Me he'rt grew strang when maist ootmoucht[3]
B' thinkan on me lovan wife –
    That she was faus I little toucht.

'Wi' selkie folk thu's led a life!
    Awa, ye limmer slut, fae me!
I wadna hae thee for a wife
    For a' the gowd i' Christindee!'

She's whipped the chain fae the selkie's haas
    An wapéd[4] it on Oddie's croon.
'Gae, tak ye that, ye ill-tongued tyke.[5]
    An' keep it for a parting boon!'

The lady they put i' a hich hich toor
    Wi' nae sweet light t'row hole or bore.
They hae gaen her meat and water there,
    An' steeked fast the iron door.

Mistress Maria Coubister, who had the ordering of the servant girls in the palace – them that swept floors, and carried plates to and from the board, and mended hose and curtains, and lit fires and carried water – Mistress Coubister had liberty to be present at whatever music or interlude chanced to be performed in the great hall; not entirely present,

---

[1] Throwing away.   [2] Darkest.   [3] Exhausted.
[4] Swung it down.   [5] Hound.

among ladies and lawyers and churchmen – that would be too presumptuous – but lingering about the main door, in all the draughts, half in the lighted hall and half in the long dark corridor, a permitted unacknowledged presence.

Mistress Coubister had been standing at the curtain, entranced, ever since the beginning of the ballad. This Corston the ballad singer had a rare talent indeed, a thing you would never guess from the way he blew his nose in his sleeve and slapped the buttocks of any lass that bent to lay peats on the kitchen fire.

> Ba loo, ba loo, me bonny bairn,
>   Ba loo lillie, ba loo lay,
>   Sleep thu, me peerie bonny budo . . .

What tenderness, when Corston sang that! – as if he had momently changed sex, and was entered into the secret estate of motherhood, and understood all its sweetnesses and pains . . . And then again, when the 'grimly gest', San Imravoe, the seal-man, stood at her bed foot and spoke, the strangeness of that dialogue, as Corston uttered it, sent cold gules down Mistress Coubister's back. But most entrancing of all it was when Odivere had killed the seal-child and confronted his wife with the gold chain from about its neck, his own parting gift to her – then Corston had to be two distracted persons at once, Odivere and the lady; he had to present them shifting up and down separate scales of emotion, in stark conflict one with the other, yet making a harmony of their bitter interchanges. How skilfully Corston had managed it, better than any flute and viol – the sudden flame of suspicion in Odivere, his wrath held in a deadly control at the start, then his loud grief and outrage and wounded pride at being a cuckold, and last his horror at the unnatural coupling; and all this while his spirited lady fought back, flung his infidelities in his teeth, flashed at him like a cat whose kitten has been taken from her untimely.

> She's whipped the chain fae the selkie's haas
> An' wapéd it on Odie's croon.
> 'Gae, take ye that, ye ill-tongued tyke,
> An' keep if for a parting boon!'

'Well done!' cried Mistress Maria Coubister from the hall door; though whether her praise was for the Lady Odivere, or for Corston the poet, or for both together, she could not well have said.

Flushed faces looked round at her.

Mistress Coubister bit her lip and slipped behind the curtain; she would hear the rest of the ballad from the darkness of the corridor . . . That Corston would have pig's trotters with stewed apples for his supper that night, yes, and whatever red wine was left over, in the oldest silver cup. She would see to it.

> The Ting[1] has passed her awfu' doom,
>   That for her fauts an' sinfu' deed,
> She 'sud be taen an' brunt tae asse
>   Withoot or mercy, or remeed.

> 'Aloor, aloor, the dolefu' day!
>   Aloor! what am I born tae see?
> I' the red-hot fire I man be burnt!
>   O waes me he'rt an' waes me.

> 'O gin me faither been i' life
>   He wad hae doorly focht for me.
> Deid mither's gest will thu no come
>   An' set thy dolefu' dochter free?

> 'When I lay on thee cother[2] breest
>   An' thu thee peerie bairn did rus,[3]
> Thu little thocht thy bonny bairn
>   Wad be a cinder i' the asse!'

[1] Assembly.　　[2] Comfortable.　　[3] Praise.

171

Then up and spak San Imravoe
　　An' a lood and wallie cry gaed he;
'Ye selkie folk, tae Norowa
　　Ca'[1] a' the whal's i' the Nort Sea!'

The day before that lady fair
　　Was tae be brunt wi' muckle woe
A cry was raised aroond the ha,
　　'Whal's, whal's, i' ilka bay and voe!'

That Odivere an' a' his men
　　Ran tae the ca' wi' muckle speed,
An' there was rowin', rootin', yowlin'.
　　An' noise that micht hae raised the deid.

They rowed an' rooted a' the day
　　But never a whal' got for their pains
An' i' the mirkin[2] home they gaed
　　Wi' sweean laevs an tiftan banes.[3]

An' when that they cam tae the ha'
　　They got a gluf,[4] ye may be sure,
For ilka door stood open wide,
　　An' the door o' the toor lay on the floor.

An' they ran up, and they ran doon,
　　An' glower'd aboot wi' a' their e'en.
The lady fair was clean awa
　　An' never mair b' mortal seen.

An' Odivere's a lanely man
　　An' weary o' his sicker skathe.[5]
An' aye an' sair he rues the day
　　He ever took the Odin aith.

Tae menye–singers[6] t'anks we gae,
　　Tae menye–singers drink we a'.

[1] Drive.　　[2] First darkness.　　[3] Smarting palms and aching bones.
[4] Shock.　　[5] Hard fate.　　[6] Wandering singers.

172

Wur foys they wur no worth a strae
Without their songs an' ballans bra'.

The ballad was over. The poet bowed across the clapping hands to the earl, and delicately advanced his right hand, palm upwards. The earl nodded to Master Baillie the factor, and Master Baillie took a silver coin from the leather pouch tied round his middle and put it formally in the poet's wavering palm. Corston winced as if the hound had bitten his fingers – he had expected a crown, not a shilling – and turned towards the door like a prince that had thrown a fistful of pearls into a pigsty.

Little Alysoun – a girl with a lamp at each side of her – went through the long corridor to the earl's bed-chamber. The ballad had set all her nerves quivering; she would not have ventured into that corridor alone for a king's ransom. She hoped the earl would not be long in coming to bed. Seenie laid a peat on the fire, Ruth began to unbutton Alysoun's dress, Agnes poured scented water in the basin for her bath, and then a little milk.

All the women had left the hall now. A new flagon of wine was brought. The earl and the two canons and the sheriff and the factor sat round the table. Master Baillie filled pewter cups for all except Master Lorimer the sheriff. If a pitchfork had been placed across Canon Fulzie's face you might have held out your hand to the bars of that furnace.

'Oh, very good,' said Master Malachi Lorimer, the sheriff, and poured a splash of well water into his cup, 'a douce interlude, a diversion to make the women sleep with little smiles on their faces, a well-turned comedy indeed . . . God forbid I should end such a pleasant evening with a douche of cold water. Yet it is no light laughing matter, the subject of the poem we heard tonight. The simple truth is this, the lord Odivere and his lady were necromancers. Odivere himself was but lightly tainted with witchcraft – he had taken the

Odin oath, that is to say, in order to win the woman he lusted after, he had been present at the offspring of a Black Mass and made his petition to Satan; which petition, as the rhyme said, was granted, but in such a dubious and equivocal fashion that the outcome set his teeth on edge.

'It will not be a hidden matter to you, Canon Fulzie, that such hellish things happen. What they principally do, the satan worshippers, is this – they coerce some wayward priest, or one that has been unfrocked (but yet has the power to his dying day to transubstantiate bread and wine), and him they have to officiate in their sacrifice. What insults and degradations they offer to the sacred Body of Christ, in order to ingratiate themselves with their own dark lord, I tremble to think; but stories are told to me, and I know houses in this parish where the rites have been performed . . . Since the old religion was lately put down, a hell-committed priest is harder and harder to find (though you, Canon Fulzie, and you too, Canon Grant, being Romish originally in your ordination, could if you were so minded lend yourselves to these abominations – the holy crucifix hanging upside down at the wall, the black candles, the *Pater Noster* chanted backwards). To such a blasphemous sacrifice this Odivere went, to gain his woman.

'Odivere, as I said, was a mere novice, a catechumen. The woman, however, this Norwegian lady, was steeped in witchcraft to her eyes, nothing of all its black ritual was hidden from her, she was so deep in its mysteries that she had gotten a succubus to lie with her, a demon that could take the form of beast or man at will. What did she want with sweethearts, such a one, when night after night she lay wrapped in huge burning animal lust? It tells us, early in the poem, that she sent them all packing, all the boys who came to woo her, with their delicate speech and paltry members; and little wonder.

'This coupling of seals with human creatures is no new

thing. The stories the crofters tell each other on a winter's night are thick with such bestiality; and they go beyond mere story-telling, they relate events that happened to their neighbours and cousins. I will take you along this shore of Birsay and I will show you a man in a croft whose grandmother lay with a selkie in a cave. Seeded, she bore sea-fruit. And furthermore I will show you a group of bairns in a Hamnavoe close that had a mermaid, a salt-water devil, for mother. Yes, their father in his young lustihood took over his threshold a stranger that no person native in the parish had seen before, a shy silent lass; and this young fisherman tells the old man and the old woman, his parents, that she is a foreigner he has saved from a shipwreck, and out of charity they must shelter her.

'So, continually, make not a doubt of it, the hell-seed is sown among the generations of men.

'Witchcraft twists every blessing into its stark opposite.

'You will have observed, for example, the constant interchange of gold in the poem, a chain and a ring and coins. A great hoard of emotion may be stored in a simple token. Love, though absent, though wayward and feeble, still gleams on neck and finger – in the end it will return to its pure precious beginnings, like a nuptial ring rounding faithfully back upon itself, heavy and solid for ever between the third joint and the knuckle. Gold is a symbol of all that is rare and high and beautiful. What a wealth of loyalty and devotion, for example, clusters about a sceptre! Yet here, in this web of witchcraft, the gold is used only for purposes of betrayal, adultery, mockery.

'The end of the ballad makes all well, everything draws to an acceptable consummation. The gentle lady is borne off by her lover and his gentle company of sea creatures into a last felicity. A haar drifts across their diminishing sea-path.

'Nothing like that, in the divine nature of things, could possibly happen. What truly happened was this, surely: the witch was carried down by the devils she had daffed and dallied with into a torment more lasting than the brief-stake ordained by that Norwegian court-of-law – even into brimstone and the fire that knows no guttering.

'What we have been listening to all this evening is a honeytongued lie.

'You lordship and reverences, this leads me to broach a pertinent question concerning the dubious nature of poetry itself. That it is a God-ordained art allows of small doubt; did not King David harp with unction unto the Lord? Eternal truths are uttered in verse – some have called it the fair fragmented light of heaven fallen about the ways of the sons of Adam, for a part consolation to them in their state of exile. Some again have argued that a poet, mounted on the winged horse, is carried willy-nilly into the clear kingdom of truth. I am not disposed to quarrel with these aestheticians.

'But I hold that poetry can wreak no common havoc in the estate of man. How so? By enlisting itself – half beast, half angel – under the ensign of the devil; so that, while indeed according to the laws of its nature it is bound to utter truth, it utters truth in a fashion so veiled – as in this ballad – that the mind of the listener, lost in a labyrinth of happy images, knows not who or what it is; it is bewildered utterly; then round some last corner it stumbles, too late, upon rampant horn and hoof.

'Plato did well to shut the door of his city-state against that perverter of true order, the poet.

'The late change in religion – men are calling it the Reformation – has purged the kirk of its centuries-thick adhesions of image and fable. At last we have the plain word for our instruction and guidance, as Saint Peter had and Saint Paul.

'New apprehensions (as if awaiting that sign) are astir everywhere in the puritan courts and universities.

'Since Master Caxton in England with his printing press struck the rock of all knowledge, streams of enlightenment have burst forth.

'We discover almost daily new subjects for our study and edification – namely, rocks, soils, effluences, clouds, stars, the laws of light and optics and velocity and mass; to name but a few chapter-headings in the great Book of Nature that has been lying open before us, unnoticed, until now. With great reverence we must apply ourselves to a careful study of it. It will not be for us, as for the readers of plays and romances, a wallowing-in-styes; we will make a sober inventory of the whole creation, together with its workings and laws, so that we shall be able to harness these divine energies to our practical use, as God no doubt desired we should. The light of science will grow. Our children will unlock the secrets of atom and planet (as much as humanity can bear); and at the end of all it may be that we will be enabled to stand among the purest sources of power, and control them, and so endow ourselves with a material splendour that as yet we can hardly conceive of. And all this power and glory achieved not by any Mephistophilean means, but by ways acceptable to God.

'But first there must be an entire uprooting of image and fable from our minds. Until that is done the seeds of the new knowledge have no room to sprout and to flourish.

'Let the poets begin to reform themselves. Let them speak plain godly sense, like honest men, from now on.

'For the witches will be no reprieve. As if they knew their end was nigh, never have they raged in Scotland and the islands so furiously as now they do. They flaunt their mysteries openly and shamelessly. It has come almost to this, that they hawk their terrors from door to door and on the public highway.

'There are things that we must do, each in our several capacities.

'Witch fires will burn on the hills of Orkney for a many a day to come. So much I can promise you. My lord, get ready your stakes and your torches. Give credit to such grave religious mouths as report oddities, however slight, from this parish and that island. Look well where they point, the secret loyal fingers, to this or that girl, however seemingly law-abiding and chaste; for she is, more likely that not, a vessel of hell.'

The sheriff sipped the last of his water. He turned a thin look on the Earl.

The Earl rose to his feet.

ROBERT RENDALL

ONE DAY in the winter of 1946 the editor of *The Orkney Herald* sent me a book to review. It was a thin collection of poems called *Country Sonnets*, printed locally. I didn't know the author; his name was Robert Rendall.

A sizeable quantity of verse is produced in the islands and sometimes finds its way into the weekly newspapers, or is privately printed. It is mostly sad stuff, romantic yearnings, tinsel and cottonwool descriptions of crag and sea and sky, all put together without craft or wit. I opened *Country Sonnets* with small enthusiasm.

The sonnets, all in English, were soundly constructed – I saw that at once – but not very exciting. There was a kind of Wordsworthian loneliness and peace in them, without Wordsworth's soaring imagination and absolute precision of language. For example, a typical Robert Rendall line in this book was 'the ageless music of the rolling seas' – he might just as well have written 'the rolling music of the ageless seas'. You can't use language as slackly as that and get away with it.

But the sonnets had structure. They had been hewn out of

the language and chiselled with care. Here and there was a line that made me sit up:

> Compassionate Spring has set God's creatures free

and

> ... the ploughman, leaning low
> Furrow on furrow o'er the landscape makes.

Among the thirty-four poems was a handful of lyrics of a kind that had lately gone out of fashion. This new poet had supped full with the Georgian – W. H. Davies, John Masefield, Walter de la Mare, Robert Bridges – and his imitations were not very exciting; lyrics like flowers pressed thin and odourless in books:

> O say not Beauty dies unsung,
> The passing cloud, the morning star,
> The daffodil with dewdrops hung,
> All lovely transient things and young
> Somewhere remembered are.

Wandering through this Georgian garden, on page 38, I came on the sea shore and a perfect poem:

The Fisherman

> Auld Jeems o' Quoys, wha erst[1] wi' leid and line
> Keen as a whitemaa,[2] reaped the Rousay Soond,
> And in his weathered yawl a twalmonth syne
> Set lapster-creels the Westness craigs aroond,
> Nae stroke o' fortune cloured[3] wi' bluidy claa,
> Nor glow'ring daith wi' sudden tempest mocked,
> But in his wee thatched croft he wore awa'
> E'en as a cruisie[4] flickers oot unslockt.
> Nae kinsman raised, nor wife, nor weeping w'ain
> But we, his yamils,[5] this memorial stane.

I wrote the review, and a few days later received a letter of

[1] Formerly. [2] Gull. [3] Struck.
[4] Fish-oil lamp. [5] Contemporaries.

acknowledgement from the poet. Not long after that I met him in the house of Ernest Marwick, the Kirkwall historian. Robert Rendall was a small dark vivacious man; he spoke rapidly in a high plangent voice. I had been warned that he had become very deaf, but in conversation this seemed to be no handicap to him at all. He generated an enormous enthusiasm. And it wasn't only poetry he talked about (though he talked wonderfully about Virgil and the Greek Anthology) – shells came into the rather one-sided conversation, watercolour painting, the Vikings. With regard to poetry, he confessed to being very interested in 'the metrical experiments of Robert Bridges'. He looked half roguish, half daring, as he said it. That was as far as he would go – beyond that the wilderness – Eliot and Pound and Dylan Thomas were poets of a new barbarism he didn't want to know anything about. He was knowledgeable about prosody and the history of the sonnet; was working, in fact, on a book about the Scottish sonnet. I gathered that the single masterpiece in his book of poems, *The Fisherman*, was lightly regarded by him – it was a kind of by-product, a thing thrown off in an idle moment, not to be weighed in the same scale with his sonnets.

In the months that followed I pieced together information about this one-poem man, from meeting him frequently (which was always a great pleasure) and from the talk of the countryside. He was a bachelor, forty-seven years old, a partner in a Kirkwall drapery firm. His paternal ancestors had come from the island of Westray, a very religious island with more Christian denominations than any other part of Orkney. Robert had been reared as a Plymouth Brother, and he still adhered strictly to that persuasion; not only that, he was one of the sect's leading theologians, and wrote pamphlets, articles, and books to expound scripture from this extreme Calvinist point of view. He was also a leading authority on shells, a conchologist, and he was writing a book to be called *Mollusca Orcadensia*, a work of pure research. He stayed in a house in

Willow Road, Kirkwall, but also he had a yellow-painted wooden house in the village of Birsay, just above the beach. He would take the bus there on early-closing days and at weekends, with his paint-box and canvases (for he was also a painter). From his seaward-facing window rose two immense crags, Marwick Head and The Brough, with a wide sweep of shore between them. He had cuithe lines at the end of his house. He was happiest of all, I think, in Birsay; there in his childhood he had spent the long summer holidays, and first raked shells from the rockpools and, on rainy days, turned over for the first time the pages of classical poets and Norse sagas. Birsay was a sacred place to him, not in any solemn sense; but these shores and hills were the source of his purest intuitions; they carried him back beyond his own childhood to the childhood of the world. Flute and vine-leaf and temple formed a background to his varied enthusiasms. He was, every bit as much as Keats, a Greek.

One day in a Kirkwall street I met Robert Rendall. Together we went into the roseate gloom of Saint Magnus Cathedral, and climbed the stone stair into the triforium. The hangman's ladder from three centuries earlier was lying there, and also fragments of a very old pulpit. The ladder was constructed with three verticals so that two men could climb it at the same time. 'Only one climbed down again,' said Robert. The worms and the centuries had been at the pulpit. Robert wrote a poem about it.

> Here i' the sooth laft's neuks sae dim,
> Twa aald-time relics – Haad thee wits!
> A hangman's ladder twa could clim',
> A widden pulpit, geen tae bits.
>
> Whaur ither should they than in kirk
> O' guid and evil mind us a!
> Time plays, hooever, mony a quirk:
> Prelate and tief are baith awa.

In 1951 Robert Rendall's second book of poems, *Orkney Variants*, was published. A silent prayer of mine had been answered: Robert, though he hadn't turned his back completely on the Georgians, had averted his face. He had drawn up a dozen or more poems from the same well that had given us *The Fisherman* – marvellous lyrics, in the Orkney dialect, with a Greek form and purity. These were the most beautiful poems written by an Orkneyman since the Reformation killed the songs and ballads of the people:

> Look! This is Liza's but and ben,
> Wi' screen o' bourtrees tae the door,
> Her stack o' peats, her flag-roofed byre,
> Her planticru abune the shore;
> Yet 'mang her hens and hoosehold gear
> She's bruck'd aboot for eighty year.

Robert Rendall was like Wordsworth in this too, that he seemed to have little notion about what was good and what was indifferent in his own poetry. He would quote to you some turgid piece about the Orkney Earls ('scorning beneath ignoble servitude / To bow their necks' . . .) or the primula ('Primrose of Orkney! / From the great sea-cliffs / Far o'er the islands / Scatter thy seed' . . .) with as much enthusiasm as *The Twa* or *Celestial Kinsmen*:

> The winter lift is glintan doun
> Wi' tullimentan[1] stars besprent,
> As were the very heavens abune
> Clean gyte[2] wi' frosty merriment,
> Their lowan e'en are taakan tent
> O' chiels like Mansie o' the Bu
> Whase days upon the land are spent
> Ruggan[3] wi' Taurus and the Pleugh.

Another curious feature of his two volumes was this – they

[1] Glittering.   [2] Daft.   [3] Striving.

each contained a few religious pieces, nods in the direction of evangelical Christianity; as if the poet thought it might be better to mingle the gay Greek garlands with sombre cuttings from Calvin. The religious poems were not, in these early volumes, good.

Nor was Robert a good artist, though he loved to paint and draw in his spare time. He rather spoiled the appearance of his books by designing the jackets and title-pages himself; so *Country Sonnets* has for sole decoration a sheaf of ink-smudged corn, and *Orkney Variants* has its title framed with improbable seaweed, anchor, crab, starfish, Viking longship – a poorish gateway to the treasures inside.

Not long after *Orkney Variants* was published I spent more than a year in a Kirkwall hospital. Robert Rendall came to see me regularly, bringing like apples and flagons his latest enthusiasm – a drawing, a discovered shell, a plan to visit Italy. His gaiety dispelled the sombre moods that gather about a long-term patient. He would read me a fragment or draft of a new poem. He recited like an old skald, in a high piercing chant; everyone in the hospital could hear him; next morning the patients would recite over their breakfast Robert's latest:

> Lord, we are thine, the captives of Thy bow:
> Fast as we fled thine arrows laid us low.
> We found Thee Friend who feared Thee once as Foe . . .

Tuberculous patients have had worse consolation.

The contents of his third book *Shore Poems* were chanted to me as they were written. The book grew and took shape in the antiseptic air around me. When it was published in 1957 I knew most of the poems by heart. In *Shore Poems* this old Prospero had lost some of his sorcery: it contained no small miracles in dialect like *The Fishermen* and *Salt i' the Bluid* and *Cragsman's Widow*. On the other hand he brought to fruition things he had striven in vain to do up to that time. He

succeded in writing a fine religious poem called *The Title*;
that Good Friday hymn could be sung as well in a Catholic
cathedral as in a gospel hall; it is truly ecumenical, it is for the
whole household of the faith:

> . . . Like a wounded wild gazelle,
> Stricken sore and mortally,
> From His parchèd lips there fell
> Groans of dire extremity:
> 'Why hast thou forsaken Me –
> Christ the King of Israel?' . . .
>
> Hail we Him, Emmanuel,
> Throned upon the royal tree,
> Who in distant islands dwell;
> And from henceforth none but He
> Shall our God and Saviour be –
> Christ, the King of Israel.

And for the first time he wrote a sonnet that had not only a
cold technical finish (he had written plenty of these) but a
heart-rooted one, exulting with new green life because, not
for the first time, it had experienced winter and death: a small
resurrection. I remember the day he wrote *Renewal*. He visited
me twice that day in my small hospital ward. In the afternoon
I could see that he was troubled and preoccupied. His talk
didn't come in quick enthusiastic gushes, as usual; there were
long silences while he gazed abstractedly, from under bushy
whorls of eyebrow, at the wintry fields outside. Then before
he left he read me the first version of the sonnet, written that
morning, a structure full of blanks and queries and confusions.

Late in the evening he came back, I think after visiting
hours. His face was flushed, his eyes glittered, he was breathless
from hurrying up the steep hill, his hands trembled as he
opened his wallet and unfolded the typewritten sheet.

Look how my autumn leaves from green to gold
    Burn in their frosty fire. Tissue and vein
    Shiver and curl to ash: no flowers remain
On withered stem, or from the patient mould
Draw breath and on life's tree their fans unfold.
    Twice has my summer pride waxed high; now wane
    The gentle influences of the rain,
The sun, the earth: and death comes, dank and cold.
But fast inscalloped in the undying root,
    Constant beyond all change of sky or soil,
Lies fenced the mystery of the living shoot –
    Green involutions of the mind. No toil
    Attends their weaving. Ah, would they uncoil
Again from that inmost core, leaf, stem, flower, fruit.

In the last ten years of his life we didn't see so much of each other. Occasionally we met in a Kirkwall street; he would tell me that he hadn't written any poems for a long time, only a few *haikus*, imitations of those brief Japanese kennings. He was busy with other things; with his book *Orkney Shore*, that mingles autobiography with all the minutely observed life of beach and rockpool; with his theological books, which struck me as being cold dutiful exercises. He presented me with a copy of one, *History Prophecy and God* – I struggled through five pages of the alien stuff, then gave up. I always feared he might ask me, next time we met, what I thought of it. But he was a man of tact; he knew that in these matters we were very far apart; and so a delicate silence was observed.

In 1965 he became very ill and lay between life and death for months in an Aberdeen hospital. We thought he had seen his last of Orkney. But the living shoot uncoiled again. He was able to return to Orkney, to St Peter's House in Stromness, a hospice for the elderly and the convalescent. When I visited him there he was thinner but he still laughed and chattered like an excited boy. He had laid in a store of novels for his winter reading. He intended to make another collection of poems – a much smaller one, for now he wrote only rarely. He formed a fast friendship with his Stromness neighbour, Ian MacInnes the artist, and in his studio at Thistlebank Ian MacInnes painted a striking portrait of the pensive mature scholar-poet. On the face of it no two men could have been more different, yet Robert found a new happiness in the gay radical atmosphere of the MacInnes household. On Sundays he attended the Brethren meetings in the Gospel Hall. He sent his few last poems, *The Hidden Land*, to the printer, and dedicated the book to Edwin Muir. He recorded his poems on tape for the English Literature students of Stromness Academy. He was delighted when two of his poems (not his best ones, unfortunately) were included in the new *Oxford Book of Scottish Verse*. That last year of his life was very like a fulfilment.

In the early summer of 1967 his illness turned on him again. I went one afternoon with Ernest Marwick to see him in Eastbank Hospital. He was very thin and weak, and he was lying in the same small ward that I had lain in fourteen years previously. Ernest brought him, fresh from the press, copies of a pamphlet Robert had written some time before about the Orkney Antiquarian Society. He struggled up in bed; he gestured towards his biro (for now he was beyond articulate speech) and he wrote 'with compl^{mts}. RR' on a copy and gave it to me. His mind had been ranging among old half-forgotten things; now he remembered seeing London slum children coming back from a day in the country with their hands full of wild flowers. He read, with great labour, the poems he had just written about them.

> *On a London Street*, 1932
> Faded flowers in fist,
> A chain of slum children
> From summer fields long missed.

Not now can squalor stain
The pure bright image
Of that fair green domain.

In mute defiance
Young eyes have glimpsed
God's glory in dandelions,

His miracle of leaf and blade,
Bud and blossom,
All that He has made.

One fine day Ian MacInnes wrapped him in blankets and carried him into his car and drove him round the familiar roads. Summer was wakening everywhere. That was the last time his eyes saw the islands.

A few days later he was dead – gathered, with the wondering children, among endless fields and flowers.

In a *haiku*, the last poem in his last book, he wrote his epitaph. He united his labours as poet, naturalist, archeologist, merchant, preacher to the work of the crofter-fisherman who hauls his boat high and secure on the beach for the winter:

Hand on gunwale – to the noust
haul this weathered yawl:
there leave her, safely housed.

6

THE WATCHER

A PLAY

THE WATCHER

Scene: Hamnavoe, a fishing town in Orkney.
   A house in a steep close above the sea, among a huddle of
   other houses.
Characters:
   Samuel Innertoon, a cobbler
   Margit, his wife
   Babs Seatter, a neighbour woman
   Michael
   Sir Robert Pollexfen, the Laird
   His servant
   Jock Seatter ⎫
   Tom Skaile ⎪
   Ally Wards ⎬ the crew of the fishing boat 'Tern'
   Amos Cutt ⎪
   Women ⎭
   Children

SCENE 1

   *The interior of the cobbler's house. A work-bench at one end of
   a bare room with a flagstone floor and a window of small scoured*

*panes looking over the harbour and the islands. A cradle near the
fire.*

*Margit, the cobbler's wife, is peering out through the window;
Babs Seatter, the woman from next door, enters carrying a pair
of heavy boots.*

BABS (*shrill as a seagull*): Margit –

MARGIT (*forefinger at lips*): Quiet . . . the bairn . . .

BABS: What is it, Margit? What are you looking at?

MARGIT: A disgrace! A shame and a disgrace! The crew of the
'Tern', all drunk, every man. They're leaving 'The White
Horse' and they're making a stagger for the pier.

BABS: Jock's among them, I warrant.

MARGIT: Yes, he is.

(*A pause.*)

BABS: Is Samuel not in?

MARGIT: He's out on business . . . What's that you have in
your hand?

BABS: Jock's boots.

MARGIT: You'll be wanting Samuel to sole them.

BABS: Yes.

MARGIT (*tartly*): Take them elsewhere. Mend them – you
haven't *paid* for them yet.

BABS: Poor catches, Margit, poor landings. They'll get a good
haul tonight. Then you'll get your money.

MARGIT: Jock Seatter can afford to drink. If you're poor, so
are we. No money, no mending. Take them somewhere
else.

BABS: Jock'll have to fish with wet feet then . . . (*At the door,
inquisitive as a gull in a bin.*) Samuel will be along at the
lawyer's paying his rent, the way it's Michaelmas.

MARGIT: No.

BABS: He'll be seeing the minister about the christening of
peedie Inga, bless her.

(Inga is the hidden flutter of breath in the cradle.)

MARGIT: No, he's buying coats for the bairns.

BABS: Five winter coats – that'll pull his purse!

MARGIT: There's folk in Hamnavoe owe Samuel for cobbling. He'll collect his debts first, then he'll buy the coats.

BABS: He's a long time, isn't he? . . . I'm saying nothing, mind, but there's more drinkers in Hamnavoe forby Jock and the crew of the 'Tern'.

(Margit says nothing.)

Maybe Samuel's in 'The White Horse' too.

MARGIT *(angry)*: God help him if he is!

BABS: Listen.

(A lift and lurch and fall of song in the close outside.)

SAMUEL: 'Andrew Ross an Orkney sailor
      Whose sufferings now I will explain
      While on a voyage to Barbadoes
      On board the vessel Martha Jane.'

(Samuel comes in, his face flaming like a forge.)

SAMUEL: Well, here I am. Margit, there'll be snow before night . . .

(He begins to intone again.) 'The mate and captain – '

MARGIT *(quietly)*: Where's the coats?

SAMUEL: Patience, lass. I have a story to tell.

MARGIT *(with rising anger)*: Story? A story won't keep your bairns warm in the snow. I said, where's the coats?

SAMUEL *(to Babs)*: How are you, Babs Seatter? Jock's sea-boots for mending. Set them down there, on the floor. I'll put a good thick sole on them. Come back on Saturday.

MARGIT *(to Samuel)*: Did you collect your debts?

SAMUEL: I got five shillings. Everybody's poor this winter, a bad harvest on top of the bad fishing.

MARGIT (*holding out her hand*): Give me the money.

SAMUEL: Hold on, woman. It was that cold I went to 'The White Horse' for a dram, to warm me.

BABS (*nodding*): Just that.

SAMUEL: I met one or two farmers. The crew of the 'Tern' were there. I saw Jock, Babs. You ken the way it is, one drink leads to another.

MARGIT (*raging*): You're a beast, Samuel Innertoon! You've drunk everything. There's not a black penny in the house.

SAMUEL: The Lord will provide.

MARGIT: What will we do for milk and coal and bread at the week-end? Tell me that.

BABS: I'll just be off. (*Babs wings off through the door, delighted, a gull crop-full of scandal.*)

MARGIT: What came of the coat you had on this morning? A poor patched thing, God kens. Did you sell it for drink too?

SAMUEL: Margit, be patient till I tell you.

BABS (*rushing in, skirling*): Ah – h – h – h!

MARGIT: What's wrong?... (*Frightened.*) Bar the door, Samuel.

BABS: There's a *thing* out there.

SAMUEL: There's nothing to be frightened of. Listen. Just listen now. I met a poor man, a stranger, and I took him home with me. He's ill, exhausted, clean done.

MARGIT: A stranger? What kind of a stranger?

SAMUEL: I'll take him in now to the fire before he perishes.

(*Samuel goes out.*)

MARGIT: God help us, tramps and tinkers next!

(*Samuel comes back, a young man behind him. He has Samuel's coat on, nothing else. He stands near the door, half turned away.*)

SAMUEL: You're all right now, Michael. They're good folk

here. They have tongues, that's all . . . (*To Margit.*) He says his name's Michael.

MARGIT: Where does he come from? Ask him that.

SAMUEL: He's a stranger.

MARGIT: Why is he naked? That's shameful . . . (*She turns to Michael.*) You can't bide here. Understand that. We're poor folk.

SAMUEL: Not so poor we can't give him a bowl of soup. Come on, lass, I'm hungry. Put broth and bread on the table.

MARGIT (*ladling out the broth*): He'll go after this soup. What do we know about him? He might be a criminal. He'll not sleep in this house, that's sure. He might cut our throats on the night.

BABS: God help us!

SAMUEL: Talk sense, woman. Just look at him. There's no harm in him at all . . . Take in that chair to the table, Michael . . . I found him against the kirk wall, between 'The White Horse' and here. There he lay humped like a sheep in a blizzard. At first I thought he was just another drunk. Then I saw the bundle of white flesh. I was feared, I hurried on past! Then in Graham Place I thought shame – I turned and I went back along the street. There he was, still. He was grey with cold, woman. I was warm enough – I had a good bead of 'White Horse' whisky in me. So I puts my coat over him. And I gets him to his feet. And here we are.

MARGIT: Where does he come from? What does he do for a living? Has he told you that?

BABS: I better go home and get the fire lit. Jock'll be back in the early hours.

(*But first she will tattle this news in three or four closes.*)

SAMUEL: Take up your spoon, Michael. Sup your broth. (*He bows his head.*) The Lord make us truly thankful for what we're about to receive.

(Samuel and Michael dip their bread in the soup.)

MARGIT *(railing)*: Maybe you'll be satisfied, Samuel Innertoon, the day we're all in the poor-house.

SAMUEL: Her mother's name was Meg Rattle. Pay no attention.

MICHAEL *(rising to his feet, not yet having broken bread)*: This is not the place.

SAMUEL *(angrily to Margit)*: Think shame, woman. You've driven him from the door. He'll get his death in the snow.

(Michael's hand is at the sneck of the door.)

MARGIT *(to Michael, uneasily)*: I'm sorry. Sit down. Finish your soup.

(Michael smiles for the first time. His smile is like a kindling of sticks in a cold empty place. Samuel and Michael sit again at the table. They dip their bread and eat.)

SAMUEL: Are you feeling better now, Michael?

MICHAEL: Yes.

(Margit lights the paraffin lamp.)

SAMUEL: You could bide here for the night. You could sleep outside in the shed, where the coal is and the dog. It's warm enough, straw and a blanket.

MARGIT *(still uneasy)*: One night only.

SAMUEL: No, Michael. For as long as you like. Have you a trade?

MICHAEL: No.

SAMUEL: We must all work. Me, I'm a cobbler. Would you help me among the boots?

MICHAEL: Yes.

SAMUEL *(pointing to a patched shirt drying at the fire)*: I have two shirts. You wear that one till you earn enough to buy a new one.

(There is a noise of children in the close outside. Michael puts down his spoon and listens.)

MARGIT: The bairns home from the school . . . *(She goes to the seaward window.)* It's started to snow. The wind's rising too. God help them on the sea.

(Margit puts more bread and plates on the table.)

The 'Tern' 'll catch nothing in this blizzard.

SCENE 2

The same room, fifteen months later.

There is a change – the place is brighter and altogether more workmanlike. There is an ordered row of shoes and boots for mending where before there was only a scattering. There are rolls of leather against the wall. There are some ornaments – a clock, a ship-in-a-bottle, a pair of china dogs – on the mantel-shelf.

An afternoon in spring.

Samuel is stitching a skin. Margit is tidying the hearth.

Babs Seatter puts her head round the door.

BABS: I won't be long, I seen him out at the pump, so thinks I, I'll come when he isn't here, he's that unchancy, that Michael or whatever you call him.

MARGIT: Come in.

BABS: Not to bide, no. Jock's at home.

SAMUEL: Not fishing? A fine day like this.

BABS: The 'Tern' hasn't caught one sillock since Sunday. Furled at the pier like a whitemaa. No, but they scraped up enough for a pint in 'The White Horse'.

SAMUEL: That's bad.

BABS: And now this . . . *(She takes a letter from her shawl.)* The rent. We couldn't pay at the term. This is the final demand, three pounds, 'Well,' says I to Jock, 'this is the end, this settles it. It's you and me for the poor-house, Jock.'

(*A brief silence.*)

SAMUEL (*taking a purse from his pocket*): Babs, last week Michael and me made five pairs of boots and two pairs of shoes.

(*He counts out sovereigns and crowns on the bench.*)

That's three pounds ten.

BABS: No.

MARGIT (*sharply to Samuel*): We're not that rich, mind on. You're not exactly Andrew Carnegie.

SAMUEL: Take it or leave it. It's a loan, woman – until such time as the 'Tern' drives a school of blue whales in front of her into the harbour of Hamnavoe.

BABS: I'm a proud woman. (*She picks up the money all the same.*)

SAMUEL (*turning over the skin he is working at, half in wonderment and half in irritation*): A devilish job! I wish Michael was here.

BABS (*shuddering*): That man – he gives me the grues. He gives me the shakes and the shudders, squatting like a trow in his corner.

MARGIT (*sharply*): Don't you say a word against Michael, woman. We can never repay Michael for what he's done for us.

SAMUEL: That's no word of a lie. Michael's a marvel. He picked up the cobbling in one week. That's a fact. A month and he was better at the trade than me, Samuel Innertoon, master shoemaker. They're coming now from all over Orkney for their footwear. I had the Provost of Kirkwall last week. And the major of the Volunteers on Tuesday. A lucky day for me when I found Michael in the snow.

(*Michael comes in, carrying a bucket of water.*)

BABS: I'll be off.

SAMUEL: I'm stuck, Michael.

(*Michael puts down his pail and goes and looks down at the work Samuel has on his knees.*)

The Norwegian skipper's boots.

(*Babs goes out, golden-fisted.*)

It's walrus skin, he said. Can you do anything with it, Michael? I never in my life worked with walrus skin.

MICHAEL: Yes.

(*Sound of hooves and wheels on the cobbles of the street above.*)

SAMUEL: Good strong ploughman's boots, that's my line.

(*Michael sits on the stool in the dark corner. He examines the walrus skin, pulls it, flexes it, fashions it. Then he takes his knife.*)

BABS (*tripping and tumbling back in*): O Lord!

MARGIT (*sharply*): What now, woman?

BABS: Margit listen. There's a coach outside. It's stopped at the head of the close. A black and silver coach and two horses like silk!

SAMUEL: Not for us.

(*A loud rap at the door. Before Margit can get the door open a stout well-dressed florid man enters, let in by a man servant.*)

SERVANT: You're the shoemaker, eh?

SAMUEL (*rising*): That's right.

SERVANT (*indicating the stout man*): Sir Robert Pollexfen, the laird.

SAMUEL (*humbly and firmly*): Sir, I think I pay enough rent. I can't afford more. You raised it the year before last. Times is bad. I'm sorry. Please –

LAIRD (*to servant*): Unroll the leather.

(*The servant spreads on the bench a piece of leather.*)

You see that leather, shoemaker?

SAMUEL: Yes, your honour.

LAIRD: Feel it.

(*Samuel pinches the leather here and there.*)

What d'you think of it?

SAMUEL: It's good enough leather, sir.

LAIRD: Good enough! God damn it, it's the finest leather procurable. Spanish leather. I bought it from the tanner in Edinburgh. D'you know how much it cost me? Three guineas.

SAMUEL: Three guineas!

LAIRD: Three guineas. Well look here, d'you know what I want you to do? You see this foot of mine? It's got gout in it. Too much claret and grouse, the medico says, but that's beside the point. I'm tired of having boots that go to pieces on my feet after a few weeks, and hurt like hell into the bargain. I've heard about your skill, Innertoon. I want you to make me a pair of comfortable walking boots that'll last a year at least. Now, d'you think you could do that for me?

SAMUEL: An anxious job, sir, working with leather like that. I'd be feared of spoiling it.

LAIRD: Spoil it – God help you if you did! On the other hand, cobbler, if you do a good job, I'll see that you're well paid. I don't haggle over ha'pennies. Now tell me, will you do the work or won't you?

SAMUEL (*turning his head*): Michael?

(*Michael nods.*)

SAMUEL: I'll do it.

LAIRD: Good man. No need to measure me. Here's the pattern, follow it exactly . . . (*The servant sets the pattern on the bench. The laird nods towards Michael.*) Who's this fellow?

SAMUEL: My workman. He'll sew the boots.

LAIRD: Will he? (*To Michael*). See you make a good job of them, Jack. Strong boots, wide fitting, comfortable, to last me a year. I'm a lot of the time on the hill with my gun.

(*Michael is looking past the laird into a corner of the room. He smiles for the second time – a momentary brightness like butter-cups over a grave.*)

What are you grinning at, eh? Just drop everything and get on with my boots. I want them for the weekend.

MICHAEL: Sir, tonight. (*He lays aside the Norwegian boots and sets to work on the new leather with his knife.*)

LAIRD (*to his servant*): Right. Come on. (*He mops his brow.*) Damned hot in here.

SAMUEL: Good day to your honour.

(*The manservant follows the laird out.*)

Well. I don't ken should we have taken the work or no. He's the kind that's never pleased ... One thing I do ken, Michael will make him good boots.

BABS (*thrilled*): Fancy that, the laird in this house, Sir Robert! O Lord!

MARGIT: I don't think I like it either.

BABS: He had a face like a sunset, Lord, what grandeur! It took more than one bottle of whisky to paint that nose on his face.

MARGIT: A kind of darkness in the room when he was here.

(*Michael works away, paying no attention.*)

SAMUEL: Supposing we spoil the leather ... (*He sits down on the bench and takes up a common boot.*) He owns all Hamnavoe, every clod and stone. He could turn us on the road like tinkers (*snapping his fingers*), just like that. He has the power of life and death, that man.

MARGIT: Three guineas – lovely leather it must be, to cost all that money! (*She crosses over and watches Michael at work – then suddenly she cries out. Samuel rises to his feet. Michael goes on working.*)

Michael, for God's sake!

SAMUEL: What's wrong?

MARGIT: Look man – Michael's sewing slippers!

SAMUEL (*blanched*): Slippers! Michael, what ails you? (*He rises from the bench and goes over to Michael.*) It was boots he wanted, for shooting grouse on the hill. The leather's ruined. So are we too, most like.

MARGIT: There's nothing surer. He owns the very air we breathe.

(*Michael goes on sewing.*)

SAMUEL: Well, it can't be helped. It's strange, though. I've never kent Michael to make a mistake before. Never.

MARGIT: You'll have to answer for it yourself, Michael. Samuel's not to blame.

(*A knock at the door.*)

SAMUEL: Who's this now?

MARGIT: It's the same knock as last time. (*In a panic.*) Hide the leather. Make some excuse.

SAMUEL: Be quiet, woman.

(*Michael goes on sewing. Samuel resolutely opens the door. The laird's manservant steps inside; his face white and beautiful and branded with a flash of truth.*)

SERVANT: I'm back again, Mr Innertoon.

SAMUEL: Is anything wrong?

SERVANT: Very much so, I'm afraid. Sir Robert is dead.

SAMUEL: Dead!

SERVANT: He died in his coach. On the street, outside the inn. A stroke. Her ladyship sent me back to you at once.

SAMUEL: What does the lady want?

SERVANT: Instead of the boots, her ladyship wants you to make a pair of slippers.

SAMUEL: Slippers!

SERVANT: Yes, for the remains. Sir Robert will be buried in them.

(*Samuel takes the two leather shapes from Michaels' lap and shows them to the servant.*)

That's quick work!

SAMUEL: We're always ready to oblige. I'll have them sent to the undertaker's this evening.

SERVANT: Do that. And send your bill to the lawyer. You'll be paid promptly. Good-day. (*He touches his cap and goes out.*)

SAMUEL: Good-day.

(*A long pause.*)

MARGIT: Michael, did you ken that man was going to die?

(*Michael nods.*)

What way did you ken?

MICHAEL: I saw the angel of death standing at his shoulder.

(*Another pause. Margit and Samuel look at each other. Michael goes on sewing the shoes of death that will never know sun or rain or grass or any dance whatever.*)

SCENE 3

A June night, some time later. Wind at the door and in the chimney. Samuel, Margit, Michael, and five children are at a low fire. Samuel is reading from the big family bible, with some difficulty.

SAMUEL: 'For he shall give his angels charge over thee, to keep thee in all thy ways. They shall bear thee up in their hands, lest thou dash thy foot against a stone.' Amen. (*He closes the Bible.*) (*To the children.*) Go to your beds.

203

(Margit shepherds the children to their room.)

They'll need a good angel out there this same night, the men on the boats. Listen to that wind.

MARGIT *(returning)*: The herring boats are in a while ago, thank God.

SAMUEL: Me, I'm not half thankful enough. The Lord's been good to this house. Michael, did I tell you they want me for a magistrate? Me, that was the poorest man in Hamnavoe five years ago, when you first knew me. Baillie Innertoon . . . I had eight hundred and thirty-six pounds fourteen shillings and twopence in the Bank last Saturday . . . I got a letter from Glasgow this morning addressed to Samuel Innertoon, *esquire*.

MARGIT: Changed days, right enough.

(A sudden rally of wind. Ornaments rattle on the mantelshelf. The house shudders.)

Listen to the gale!

SAMUEL: The 'Tern', did she go out this morning?

(He slides the wooden bolt in the door.)

MARGIT: Jock and Tom and Ally and Amos were still in 'The White Horse' at dinner time. A poor shiftless crew.

SAMUEL *(rising)*: Go to bed, woman. I'll just come. Michael, will you put out the light?

(Michael nods.)

(Margit goes into the ben-room.)

Goodnight, Michael.

MICHAEL: Goodnight.

SAMUEL: The wind's rising.

(Samuel goes into the ben room. Michael crosses to the window and looks out over the scrolled and silver sea. There is a loud battering at the door.)

BABS (*outside*): Samuel! Open the door. Margit!

(*Michael stays where he is, at the window. Enter Samuel from the inner room, in drawers and flannel shirt and bare feet.*)

SAMUEL: What's that? . . . Michael, why don't you open the door?

(*Michael says nothing.*)

BABS (*outside*): Samuel! Margit!

SAMUEL: That's Babs. There's something wrong. (*He slides the bolt and the door lashes open. Babs comes in on the skirts of the gale. Samuel shoulders the door shut.*)

BABS: They're done for this time, Samuel. The 'Tern's' out west.

SAMUEL: She didn't sail.

(*Enter Margit in a long grey nightgown.*)

BABS: She sailed after tea. Their money ran done in the pub. They just wanted one box of fish, the poor men. Says Jock to Tom, 'One box, then we'll get a bottle of "Old Orkney".' And Tom says, 'Yes, that's fine.'

MARGIT: What's wrong?

SAMUEL: The 'Tern', she says.

BABS: They're all dead for sure. I might have kent. The farmer of Breckness rode in. The 'Tern' was in terrible trouble, he said.

SAMUEL: (*to Babs*): Be quiet woman. They're sheltering somewhere. . . . (*To Margit*): Light the lantern. I must get down to Ness, to the lifeboat shed. (*He takes an oilskin from the hook and puts it on.*) Are you sure this is true, Babs? I understood the boats were all in. (*To Michael.*) Will you come, Michael? The lifeboat's short of crew.

MICHAEL: No.

(*Samuel, the lantern in his fist, opens the door. The night howls. Samuel goes out. Babs runs after him. The close is full of lanterns. Margit closes the shuddering door.*)

MARGIT: Where did she say the 'Tern' was, Michael?

MICHAEL: Out west.

MARGIT: A bad coast to be with a westerly gale. (*She puts on her coat over her nightgown.*) I hope that old fool doesn't try climbing on the crags, or anything like that. He's too old for a hero. I wouldn't put it past him ... Wind - it's a hurricane. (*She pokes up the fire.*) Come from the window, Michael. You'll see nothing from there.

(*Michael stays where he is.*)

Four of them. There's Jock, Babs' man, a poor drunken thing. There's Tom Skaill, with six mouths to feed and another one coming before winter. There's Ally Wards, three times saved in the Salvation Army and three times a backslider. And there's Amos Cutt, never once sober since New Year, a sorrow to his old mother. (*She shakes her head.*) Still they're all men.

(*Michael says nothing. At the window, he is just outside the frail circle of light from the paraffin lamp.*)

MARGIT: What times does the clock say. Michael? Passing two. It should be getting light soon. Who would have thought there would be a storm like this in the month of June? There's no telling. A score of boats went out this morning. There was said to be good fishing, a shoal off Suleskerry, herring. They all came back in the darkening. That's when the 'Tern' must have gone out ... The Black Craig! God kens how many boats have ended there. I mind the 'Annie Jane' ... the 'Southern' ... the 'Beautiful' ... the 'Maggie'. And that's only in my time.... The 'Beautiful' - that was the very day you came to bide here, Michael - one man was saved out of the 'Beautiful', he was three days in a cave before they found him – they still call the place Charlie's Hole, Charlie was the sailor's name. . . . Michael, what do you think, they will be lost, Jock and Amos and Tom and Ally? What are you seeing out there? . . . (*Fearfully.*) You're not seeing the angel of death again?

(*Michael bides unspeaking at the window. Time surges on, a slow black heave.*)

Tell me this then, if there's a good God in heaven, what way does he allow such things? Storm and shipwreck. I go to the kirk every Sabbath, but I'll never fathom that. They haven't done much harm to anybody. It's true, they maybe took a drink at the week-end or when they had a good catch. But other than that they were harmless folk. There's plenty of bad folk in world, Michael, and nothing comes on them at all. No, they seem to prosper. What way, if there's a God, does he allow it? He has only to stretch out his hand. . . . (*She rises and looks over at Michael.*) Michael, you could save them if you liked! (*Michael doesn't reply. Margit returns to her chair.*) No, I'm sorry I said that. Pay no attention to a foolish old wife. But would you not be of more use down at the shore – not just biding there at the window, Michael, saying nothing?

(*Michael still says not a word. Samuel enters in a roar of darkness. His oilskin steams. His lantern is out.*)

SAMUEL: It's no use. (*He forces the door shut.*)
MARGIT: What news?
SAMUEL: Nothing. We saw nothing. Nothing, woman. (*He puts down the lantern on the floor.*) God knows. We searched the whole coast as far as Marwick Head. There was nothing.

MARGIT: Where's Babs?

SAMUEL: At Warbeth with the other women. The tide turns in an hour. Then there might be something to find.

MARGIT: God kens, there were some poor women in this place – poorer than gulls – between drink and torn nets. What will Babs do now, Samuel?

SAMUEL: They could be sheltering – Yesnaby, maybe, though we took a look in there too.

MARGIT: Babs could live here, in the attic. We have room.

SAMUEL: (*vehemently*): No! That tongue of hers – it would cut me to pieces like an old rag – I could never endure it. She won't bide here, I can assure you of that. . . . (*He notices Michael at the window.*) Hello, Michael, is that you? (*A long silence.*) Have you been there all the time, Michael? . . . (*To Margit.*) Well now, I'll clean out the attic. Babs can bide here right enough. For a week or two, till she gets a place somewhere. Nothing to stop her. You'll get used to anything.

MARGIT: It's getting light. (*She rises and moves to the window.*) There's some women at Ness.

SAMUEL: Woman, I'm cold. I need some toddy.

MARGIT: You and your drink. (*She brings a whisky bottle and a cup and a pot out of the cupboard.*)

SAMUEL: Well, Michael, what have you to say about this? (*He puts out the lamp – the first summer light comes grey through the window.*) This is what it is to be a fisherman.

(*Margit pours whisky into the pot and stirs a flame out of the fire with the poker and sets the pot on top of the stove.*)

MARGIT: Yes, and the wives of fishermen.

(*The wind drops so suddenly that Samuel and Margit look at each other, startled. In the new tranced silence the door opens and the four fishermen of the 'Tern' enter – Jock Seatter, Babs' wastrel; Tom Skaill, a grave bearded elderly man; and Ally*

Wards and Amos Cutt, young lazy good-natured fellows.
Michael goes back to his stool in the corner. Samuel and Margit
stand like stones.)

JOCK: Samuel, you're not saying much.

SAMUEL: Sit down, Jock Seatter, if it's you.

TOM: Margit, we've had better welcome in this house.

MARGIT (*beginning to scurry*): Sit down, Jock. Sit down, Tom.
Ally and Amos, sit down. (*She sets out chairs for them.*)
(*The four fishermen sit round the fire. Margit brings out more*
cups.)

TOM (*gravely*): We came to say, thank you, Michael.

SAMUEL: Then the 'Tern' wasn't out at all, Jock.

JOCK: She was out, Samuel. God, she was out all right.

ALLY: She was that.

AMOS (*turning to the corner*): Thanks, Michael.

JOCK: We lost creels, lines, everything. The mast's broken.
Hell knows where the rudder is. The 'Tern's' a wreck.

ALLY: Mistress Innertoon, you haven't such a thing as a drop
of whisky?

TOM: I never thought to live among waves thirty feet high.

SAMUEL: The lifeboat was out searching for you all night. It's
funny we missed you. Where did you shelter?

(*Margit brings round cups of hot sweetened whisky.*)

MARGIT (*tartly*): Ally Wards, I thought when you joined the
Salvation Army you swore never to touch drink again.
(*She turns to Jock Seatter.*) Would you stop spitting tobacco
joice on my clean floor!

(*A woman with a grey shawl comes in and stands against the*
wall.)

AMOS: A new mast and rudder – where'll we get that?

TOM: Amos, you should be glad your life's been spared, thanks
to Michael.

SAMUEL: Jock, and was it Yesnaby you were, right enough?

JOCK: The Black Craig.

SAMUEL: No.

TOM (*nodding*): We came ashore where we struck, at the Black Craig.

SAMUEL: There's no path up the Black Craig. Nobody could climb that face on a night like last night. That's impossible.

JOCK: Ask Michael.

TOM: Michael guided us to the top.

ALLY (*raising his cup*): We're very beholden to you Michael.

THE FISHERMEN (*raising their whisky*): Michael.

(*Michael bends his head over his work. He is making a pair of seaboots. An old woman in a black shawl and a young bright-haired woman come in and stand against the wall.*)

MARGIT: No. Michael was never over that door.

SAMUEL: Tell me what happened.

JOCK: A mile off Breckness the weather struck us. Everything went overboard. The sea flung us at the crags. Ally there, he started to pray.

ALLY: It was time, I thought.

TOM: We struck in the first darkness. I found myself in the water. And there suddenly was Michael, with a lantern, at the foot of the Craig, on a ledge of rock.

AMOS: That's right, isn't it, Michael?

MICHAEL: Yes. (*He smiles for the third time. . . . Legions of beings there are that exist in endless light; light their breath and substance and being. Some dwell near the pure sources; and some, equal in glory, travel on errands of love between the immaculate spheres and this dark rut. The eternal Love spoke to such a messenger, concerning the death of fishermen, that he might husband their souls like stalks of corn for the threshing-floors of Purgatory. He plummeted, but turned back soon from spindrift and wave-cry. No – it was too cruel – he would have no part in this terrible operation of Love upon the sick be-*

nighted children of men! . . . 'Thou shalt discover then on earth the three clay lamps of charity by which good men stumble heavenwards; the which vessels thou thinkest I have neglected to provide with oil, dear wayward angel.' . . . Naked upon stones he fell. Two truths from the sacred comedy of man had torn two smiles from the shuttered angel-exile. The third truth appeared now – the third lamp brimmed – and answering heaven-light welled from his lips and eyes; so that those in the room with him thought that the sun had risen clear of the hills, and shone in at the window for a moment, before the morning clouds gathered about it.)

MARGIT: Michael, you stood all night at that window.

(Babs Seatter in a grey shawl comes in and stands silent with the other women at the wall.)

SAMUEL: Woman, put more whisky on the pot. You speak too much. Well done, Michael.

MARGIT: Michael never left this house.

JOCK: Michael pulled us out of the sea, one after the other. Then he led us up the face of the Craig, to the top. We're beholden to him.

SAMUEL: Help yourselves to the whisky, men. Jock and Tom and Ally and Amos, I'm very pleased to see you. You know the man to come to when you need your boat repaired – yes, and new gear and nets. Bailie Samuel Innertoon, master shoemaker, esquire.

On the following pages are other recent paperbacks
published by Quartet Books.
If you would like a complete catalogue of
Quartet's publications please
write to us at 27 Goodge Street, London W1

PENTIMENTO
Lillian Hellman

'An irresistibly readable book' – *Cosmopolitan*

'All in all, a beautiful book' – *Daily Mirror*

Includes the story *Julia* now filmed starring Jane Fonda and Vanessa Redgrave – who won an Oscar for her performance in the film.

Autobiography £1.00

CARAVAN OF DREAMS
Idries Shah

Idries Shah has achieved world-wide recognition as one of the leading experts on Oriental philosophy and religion; in *Caravan of Dreams* he distils the essence of all his learning in a feast of stories from all over the East.

'*Caravan of Dreams* is . . . informing, instructing, entertaining, alarming, with funny and intensely painful moments, others of immediate practicality and others of extraordinary enchantment' – *New Society*

Literature/Philosophy £1.25

ALONE OF ALL HER SEX
The Myth and the Cult of the Virgin Mary
Marina Warner

In this extraordinary book, at once a feat of scholarship and a literary achievement of great beauty, Marina Warner penetrates the layers of Mariology to bring us something remarkable: a biography of the Virgin that reveals her in all her guises from human woman to Queen of Heaven.

'This is a most interesting and beautifully written book' – *The Times*

Mythology/Religion £3.95